95 Theses Project: Let's Save our Constitution

With the U.S. Constitution & The Declaration of Independence

By Bill Basaar

ISBN: 1494761270
ISBN 13: 9781494761271

The opinions given by the author are meant for debate and discussion between *We the people* of the United States in our struggle to return to a government that operates strictly under the rule of our U. S. Constitution.

Great effort was given to the correctness of the quotes. There was no access to the actual historical documents, only many trustworthy sources. After checking multiple sources, the quotes provided are certainly the written or spoken words of our Founding Fathers and the other people quoted in this document.

The 95 Theses are not intended to cause disgrace or to discredit any one person or group of people, but are to tell the world and especially the Americans to turn from their godless ways in domestic life and in the political realm.

Cover by Synergy Ninjas http://synergyninjas.com/
Nail image by Scott Robinson
Liberty Bell image by Chris Brown

The door on the cover is one of the two Columbus Doors that open into the Rotunda of the United States Capital Building from the east entrance. These solid bronze doors were designed and sculpted by Randolph Rogers between the years of 1855-1861 and installed in 1871. The images on the doors depict the significant events in the life of Christopher Columbus. The doors are 16 feet 8 inches high, 9 feet 9 inches wide and weigh 20,000 pounds.

TABLE OF CONTENTS

Author's Introduction

My Hope:
That all of *We the People* be involved in saving our Constitution

I arrived at a decisive point, in the course of time, seven years ago, when a profound impression compelled me to write *2020 Torn Asunder,* followed by *95 Theses Project: Let's Save our Constitution,* and I pray, both will have an impact for good on our nation.

When I was in the last few months of writing *2020 Torn Asunder,* I attended the Washington State Republican Convention as a delegate in 2012. After the three days of political rhetoric, I was deeply disturbed by the fact that nothing of importance was accomplished at the event. It seemed to me that the only thing accomplished was that the delegates paid money to pad the treasury of the party. I went home angry. I wanted to do something that would have a valuable impact on our nation and its politicians.

Then one day I remembered Martin Luther, a Catholic monk, who on October 31, 1517, did what was an ordinary activity of that day, he nailed his 95 Theses on the door of the Castle Church of Wittenberg. (A thesis is a proposition advanced as an argument which was the common way in those days to tell of your disagreements that were intended to start debate on the thesis.) Martin Luther's 95 theses told the Catholic Church that he strongly disputed their claim that freedom from God's punishment for sin could be purchased with money. The Catholic Church would not discuss or debate the 95 Theses, and thus, the Protestant Reformation started. In the same spirit of Martin Luther, my desire is to urge Americans into a healthy debate on our Constitution and loss of our liberties.

I started my 95 Theses with the same words and format that Martin Luther used for his 95 Theses. On the front cover of this book, I have symbolically used one of the Columbus doors that open into the Rotunda located at the East entrance of the United States Capitol Building in Washington D.C. Though I physically could not nail my 95 Theses to a door, my intent is to resemble the cathedral doors that Martin Luther nailed his 95 Theses to in 1517.

Martin Luther's actions changed the course of history and still greatly impact us today. I hope that his influence on me will in even a small way begin to change a nation of immoral people as a whole, into a virtuous people who follow Biblical principles and then elect politicians who vow to follow the U.S. Constitution as our Founding Fathers intended.

In the course of time, there comes a moment when a profound idea intrigues a person; then it begins to annoy him. Shortly thereafter, the provocative essence of the idea escalates into an urgent, life-changing circumstance that challenges him to either change his daily habits in order to fulfill the unreal idea, or stay in the norm and just be another statistic.

In all my years of living my domestic life along the sidelines of the political realm, I have quietly watched the steady encroachment of tyranny as our government creates more and more laws and regulations on everything we do; they order manufacturers how to build their products; they overburden us with more and more regulations on farming and logging, fishing and hunting and mandate what we can eat or not eat, what we can buy or not buy and what we can sell and not sell. For small or large businesses to stay in operation they must follow the complicated details of the newest regulations on tax, payroll, employee benefits, industrial and healthcare laws or they will be forced out of business by the tyrants that run our state and federal governments. *We the People* cannot freely bear arms from state to state. Our bodies are searched at the airports; our vehicles, our boats, our houses and our businesses are searched without reason and even without court orders. They treat law-abiding citizens as criminals in the name of security and trample our freedoms in the name of justice.

Most of our political leaders, corporate executives, bankers, teachers and professors, along with the so-called free press, care only for their self-interests and social agendas. Therefore, they have joined forces with the judicial system that has also become corrupted by their socialistic ideology that becomes the rule of law based upon their whims and notions or arbitrary opinions that allow the tyranny to be accepted as the norm rather than the Constitution which is the supreme law of the land.

As a whole, our nation has become an immoral and godless people. Most of us could not care less about the corrupt cronyism between politicians and business people, between state governments and the federal government, between judges and lawyers and between the courts and political operatives who are violating the Constitution.

We the People, lacking wisdom, believe that our government will automatically abide by every Article and Amendment of the Constitution. We listen to the emotional appeals of the media and politicians that pull at our heartstrings till we mindlessly swing on the end of their emotional, hypnotic pendulum, not realizing that our politicians want to create new laws and regulations that move them closer to their ultimate goal of tyranny over every aspect of the country under the pretense of following the Constitution. It is with certainty that most of the country's citizens know very little of the Constitution and are therefore, unable to help save our liberties.

In our indifference, we place all our Constitutional rights into the hands of our despotic politicians and judges who think they know what is best for us. In our ignorance we allow the only means of Constitutional interpretation to come from today's professors of law or judges. Our lazy spirits are corrupted by immorality in thoughts and actions, for to think that we can be careless about our liberties and merely trust that our politicians and judges will follow the rules of the U.S. Constitution is a dangerous act that injures every freedom-loving person in the world as well as the generations yet to come.

We must not put our faith in the politicians who desire lifetime appointments. We must not rely on talk show hosts. We must not trust the media; we must not believe the professors and judges regarding what the Constitution says and means, for most of them have power-hungry, socialistic, ideological agendas contrary to the correct rule of law that the Constitution provides.

We alone are responsible to learn about every aspect of our Constitution and our Bill of Rights. We must only trust ourselves; we must read it for ourselves, study it and teach it until everyone comes to realize that until we elect 535 Congressional members who will strictly adhere to the Constitution, we are doomed to be ruled by tyrants.

Besides reading it and studying it, I believe that the only other true source of a clear understanding of the

Constitution is through the quotes and writings of our Founding Fathers who gave us a very limited federal government. The only truest interpretation comes from those who debated, wrote and then adopted the document.

Now there is the argument, that the Constitution is a living breathing document whose interpretation changes with the ever-changing culture. This is a relativistic approach.

However, to best understand any piece of literature, one must come at it from the author's perspective. If one wants to comprehend Shakespeare, one must understand an older style of English to do so. To best understand Homer, it helps to have some concept of Greek mythology. Both Shakespeare and Homer wrote in different manners at different times in history. Nevertheless, to grasp their message it is imperative to know the meaning of their vocabulary at the time.

Thus, it is the same with the U.S. Constitution. Each word was painstakingly picked to produce an exact action and response. Our founders were absolutists, and they absolutely and resolutely wrote the Constitution and the Bill of Rights with an unchanging, precise meaning for a responsible, free people.

Therefore, I have selected numerous quotes in hopes that the ones used in my Theses will help all of us come to a better understanding of the U.S. Constitution and what the authors of the Constitution meant it to mean for all time. Perhaps it will then be realized that our politicians and judges are already ruling in an overbearing, oppressive, burdensome, tyrannical, unconstitutional manner.

Read the Constitution that is in this small book. Study the Articles and Amendments. In this document, there is also a short list of words used by our Founding Fathers during that time period of history. I have used the 1828 Noah Webster Dictionary to obtain the meanings of the words, with the intent that you will come to a better understanding of the Constitution.

Take it upon yourself to become the Constitutional expert at work, at church, at the ball field and in your neighborhood. Join me in my campaign, 'Let's Save Our Constitution.' Our liberties, our normal domestic lives and our pursuit of happiness are at stake. If we do nothing, they will soon be lost forever. We will be the generation that will be held accountable for the loss; we must vote the tyrants out of office and tell them we do not want them to have any further involvement in our government.

Included in this booklet are the Declaration of Independence and my list of equal offences that the tyrants in our federal and state governments have unconstitutionally placed upon us over the past years.

Over the decades we have gone from the Constitution's strict rule of a limited government to an unconstitutional, illegal, unlimited government under the guise of benevolence that creates a purposeful ever-expanding debt. In this scheme, *We the People* are given huge sums of aid and welfare that is a form of extortion compelling a gratuitous addicted people to vote for these same corrupt politicians who promise even greater gratuities. In this treacherous ruse both the rich and the poor have become slaves of our authoritarian government.

Yes, we have stood by and done nothing while our politicians have systematically torn asunder the Constitution. They explain away our rights with invented ideas and various lies; they say that for our safety they must make a new law; they say the Constitution is outdated, or it is a breathing, changing document, or that the Founding Fathers meant differently. And soon we allow another right to be infringed upon.

I implore you to read the following three quotes about the Constitution.

> *"On every question of construction, let us carry ourselves back to the time when the Constitution was adopted, recollect the spirit manifested in the debates, and instead of trying what meaning may be squeezed out of the text, or invented against it, conform to the probable one in which it was passed."*

Thomas Jefferson

> *"The first and governing maxim in the interpretation of a statute is to discover the meaning of those who made it."*

James Wilson
(Mr. Wilson signed the Declaration of Independence and Constitution and was an original justice of the Supreme Court)

"Today, the Constitution is our most priceless inheritance—our bulwark against encroaching tyranny. But the Constitution, which belongs to each of us and is our greatest protection, will continue to be the effective guardian of our rights only as long as each American recognizes his responsibilities and discharges them accordingly. Unless we know the Constitution...we cannot understand it...we cannot give it support necessary to preserve our liberties. If we remain in ignorance of our Constitution, how can we defend it?
Our forefathers left us a free government which is a miracle of faith—strong, durable, marvelously workable. Yet it can remain so only as long as we understand it, believe in it, devote ourselves to it, and when necessary fight for it. It is up to each one of us to keep the House of Liberty in good repair."

J. Edgar Hoover
(Mr. Hoover was the first Director of the FBI)

Our country's federal government and all state governments are on the verge of total and absolute tyranny. I am appalled at the apathy of our nation's citizens. *We the People* are the only guardians of our freedoms and liberties granted by our Constitution. I urge you to read Article I Section 8 and come to understand that Congress has ONLY eighteen duties. Yes, they are extremely limited in what they can do legally! Then note that Amendment X gives the states authority in all the domestic areas that it does not give to Congress. Carefully read Article II Section 2 & 3 and note that the President has very limited powers. Study Article III Section 2 and come to realize that the Supreme Court rulings are limited to laws that Congress passes, to treaties, to cases involving ambassadors and controversies between states. Most of my 95 Theses are connected to the Articles and Amendment X mentioned above as well as Article VI. Furthermore, as you study the meaning of the words in the vocabulary and Amendments 1, 2, 4 and 9, you will come to realize that our politicians are taking away our Constitutional freedoms.

I pray that we return to our Judeo-Christian foundation, for only a virtuous, God-fearing people can save us from the tyranny that has already eroded most of our liberties.

I pray to God that He grant us the blessings promised in the Bible if we follow His commandments. I pray that He grant us my hope that our Constitution once again is followed by our leaders as they throw off the yoke of the government's heavy, burdensome laws and taxes on *We the People.* I believe that with God's help and *We the People's* strong will to stop our unlimited government we can win back and be secure in the blessings of Liberty and again be free from the ever-grasping, overreaching tentacles of government tyranny.

95 THESES

Disputation of Author Bill Basaar
On the Power and Efficacy of Congress's
Tax and Spend Indulgences

Out of my concern for our Constitutional freedoms being taken from us by our tyrannical, political leaders, the following propositions must be discussed and debated at great lengths under the leadership of Bill Basaar; Master of Arts in Teaching with an Endorsement in History; author of *2020 Torn Asunder. We the people* must be taught and informed of the basics of the Constitution and together develop plans to save our freedoms and liberties before they are gone forever.

1. **Our right to bear arms gives *We the People* the right to carry arms freely from state to state and is not limited to small firearms, but to any firearm that the government's armed forces use; this right**

shall not be infringed upon by the cities, states, Congress or the President.
(Article I Section 8, Article VI & Amendment II)

"I ask, Sir, what is the militia? It is the whole people. To disarm the people is the best and most effectual way to enslave them."

George Mason

(Mr. Mason was one of the most frequent speakers at the Constitution Convention)

"The congress of the United States possesses no power to regulate, or interfere with the domestic concerns, or police of any state: it belongs not to them to establish any rules respecting the rights of property; nor will the constitution permit any prohibition of arms to the people;…"

St. George Tucker

(Mr. Tucker was an attorney, professor of law & judge: his writings are in Blackstone's Commentaries-1803)

"A free people ought not only to be armed and disciplined, but they should have sufficient arms and ammunition to maintain a status of independence from any who might attempt to abuse them, which would include their own government."

George Washington

"The prohibition is general. No clause in the Constitution could by any rule of construction be conceived to give to congress a power to disarm the people. Such a flagitious attempt could only be made under some general pretence by a state legislature. But if in any blind

pursuit of inordinate power, either should attempt it, this amendment may be appealed to as a restraint on both.

William Rawle

(Mr. Rawle is referring to the Second Amendment. He was appointed by George Washington as a U.S. District Attorney. He wrote: *A View of the Constitution of the U.S. of America (1829)*

"...the powers of the sword are in the hands of the yeomanry of America from sixteen to sixty. The militia of these free commonwealths, entitled and accustomed to their arms, when compared with any possible army, must be tremendous and irresistible. Who are the militia? Are they not ourselves? Is it feared, then, that we shall turn our arms each man against his own bosom. Congress have no power to disarm the militia. Their swords, and every other terrible implement of the soldier, are the birth-right of an American...the unlimited power of the sword is not in the hands of either the federal or state governments, but, where I trust in God it will ever remain, in the hands of the people."

Tench Coxe

(Mr. Coxe held sub-cabinet positions under the first four Presidents)

2. The Republican politicians merely comply with the tyrannical, unconstitutional laws of Congress under the pretense of trivial accomplishments; they are themselves tyrants and must be removed from office.

"When the righteous rule, the people rejoice; when the wicked rule, the people groan."

William Patterson

(Supreme Court Justice reminding his fellow justices in 1800)

"I believe there are more instances of the abridgement of the freedom of the people by the gradual and silent encroachment of those in power, than by violent and sudden usurpation."

President James Madison

"All governments have a natural tendency towards an increase, and assumption of power;...the people of America are not exempt from this vice in their constitution. We have seen that parchment chains are not sufficient to correct this unhappy propensity; they are, nevertheless, capable of producing the most salutary effects; for, when broken, they warn the people to change those perfidious agents, who dare to violate them."

St. George Tucker

"Guard against the postures of pretended patriotism."

George Washington

"Patriotism is the last refuge of scoundrels"

William Samuel Johnson

(Mr. Johnson was a delegate to the Constitutional Convention)

3. Most Democrats with the use of deceitful, emotional appeals and twisted, benevolent words do willfully attempt to overthrow every Article and Amendment in the Constitution, except those that benefit their plans to stay in tyrannical power forever. They are not patriots, but tyrants.

"How strangely will the tools of a tyrant pervert the plain meaning of words."

Samuel Adams

"The invasion of private rights is chiefly to be apprehended, not from acts of Government contrary to the sense of its constituents, but from acts in which the Government is the mere instrument of the major number of the Constituents."

James Madison

"The known propensity of a democracy is to licentiousness which the ambitious call, and the ignorant believe to be liberty."

Fisher Ames
(1758-1808)
(Mr. Ames was a Congressman from Massachusetts)

"Neither the wisest constitution nor the wisest laws will secure the liberty and happiness of a people whose manners are universally corrupt. He therefore is the truest friend to the liberty of his country who tries most to promote virtue, and who…will not suffer a man to be chosen into any office of power who is not a wise and virtuous man.

Samuel Adams

"The government of the United States is a definite government, confined to specified objects. It is not like the state governments, whose powers are more general. Charity is no part of the legislative duty of the government."

James Madison

4. ObamaCare is tyranny. Our government's secret is that our health care rights are to be under <u>international medical codes!</u> It is unconstitutional. Congress has no power given in the Constitution to mandate what you must purchase! When a President confers with a Supreme Court Judge in secret, what else are we to believe, but that they are joining forces against the Constitution! (Article I Section 8)

"Were the power of judging, joined with the legislature, the life and liberty of the subject would be exposed to arbitrary control, for the judge would then be the legislator. Were it joined to executive power, the judge might behave with the violence of the oppressor. The internal effects of a mutable policy...poisons the blessings of liberty."

James Madison

"It will be of little avail to the people, that the laws are made by men of their own choice, if the laws be so voluminous that they cannot be read, or so incoherent that they cannot be understood; if they be repealed or revised before they are promulgated, or undergo such incessant changes that no man, who knows what the law is today, can

guess what it will be tomorrow. Law is defined to be a rule of action; but how can that be a rule, which is little known, and less fixed?"
James Madison

"The judiciary of the United States is the subtle corps of sappers and miners constantly working under ground to undermine the foundations of our confederated fabric. They are construing our constitution from a co-ordination of a general and special government to a general and supreme one alone. This will lay all things at their feet..."
Thomas Jefferson

"Government is instituted to protect property of every sort; as well that which lies in the various rights of individuals, as that which the term particularly expresses. This being the end of government, that alone is a just government which impartially secures to every man whatever is his own."
James Madison

"(The purpose of a written constitution is) to bind up the several branches of government by certain laws, which, when they transgress, their acts shall become nullities; to render unnecessary an appeal to the people, or in other words a rebellion, on every infraction of their rights, on the peril that their acquiescence shall be construed into an intention to surrender those rights."
Thomas Jefferson

5. **A godless media, a godless judiciary, a godless government, a godless society leads to a country ruled by tyrants, not the Constitution.**

"Our Constitution was made only for a moral and religious people. It is wholly inadequate to the government of any other."

John Adams

"Without morals a republic cannot subsist any length of time; they therefore who are decrying the Christian religion, whose morality is so sublime and pure(and) which insures to the good eternal happiness, are undermining the solid foundation of morals, the best security for the duration of free governments."

Charles Carroll
(Mr. Carroll signed the Declaration of Independence)

"For avoiding the extremes of despotism or anarchy...the only ground of hope must be on the morals of the people. I believe that religion is the only solid base of morals and that morals are the only possible support of free governments."

Gouverneur Morris
(Mr. Morris was known as the 'Penman of the Constitution')

"Providence has given our people the choice of the rulers, and it is the duty, as well as the privilege and interest of our Christian nation, to select and prefer Christians for their rulers."

John Jay
(John Jay was the first chief justice of the Supreme Court)

6. **Our freedoms, our liberties and our happiness are contingent on the fact that we have no fear of our government. But when we fear the IRS, TSA, NSA**

and our border guards, we are under tyrannical controls with no recourse but to obey the order to be illegally searched or be arrested.
(Preamble, Amendments I, II, III, IV, V, VI, VII, VIII & IX)

"When the people fear their government, there is tyranny; when the government fears the people, there is liberty."

Thomas Jefferson

"It is the duty of the patriot to protect his country from its government."

Thomas Paine

(Mr. Paine wrote *Common Sense*; it inspired the patriots in our War of Independence)

"The Constitution is not a document for the government to restrain the people: it is an instrument for the people to restrain the government lest it come to dominate our lives and our interests"

Patrick Henry

(Mr. Henry was a lawyer/politician: known as an orator who argued for the Bill of Rights)

"The greatest calamity which could befall us would be submission to a government of unlimited powers."

Thomas Jefferson

7. **The Constitution prohibits Congress from usurping the people's money and giving it to the poor. This**

is the duty of the states, churches and the people. When the President and Congress provide welfare money and care of any kind, their gratuitous actions are the reasoning of tyrants.
(Article I Section 8)

"Every step we take towards making the State our caretaker of our lives, by that much we move toward making the State our Master."

Dwight Eisenhower

"Congress has not unlimited powers to provide for the general welfare but only those specifically enumerated."

Thomas Jefferson

"I cannot undertake to lay my finger on that article of the Constitution which granted a right to Congress of expending, on objects of benevolence, the money of their constituents."

James Madison
(Annals of Congress 1794)

"The government of the United States is a definite government, confined to specified objects. It is not like the state governments, whose powers are more general. Charity is no part of the legislative duty of the government."

James Madison

8. None of the Cabinet members, not one of the Czars, not even the President, not the FBI, not the ATF, not even the Justice department have the authority

to issue any new law or regulation or arrest any of *We the People;* none of the Executive branch's 7.3 million employees have the Constitutional power over any of the citizens of any state, and must not be allowed to disburse any of the country's money. (Article I Section 8, Article II)

"The means of defense against foreign danger historically have become the instruments of tyranny at home."

James Madison

"A power in the individuals who compose legislature, to fish up wealth from the people, by nets of their own weaving…will corrupt legislative, executive, and judicial public servants"

John Adams

"Do we imagine that our assessments operate equally? Nothing can be more contrary to the fact. Whenever a discretionary power is lodged in any set of men over the property of their neighbors, they will abuse it."

Alexander Hamilton

"In the first place, it is to be remembered, that the general government is not to be charged with the whole power of making and administering laws: its jurisdiction is limited to certain enumerated objects, which concern all the members of the republic, but which are not to be attained by the separate provisions of any."

James Madison

9. The Supreme Court is not the law of the land as they ruled in the case Cooper v. Aaron in 1958. (Article III Section 2)

"You seem...to consider the judges as the ultimate arbiters of all constitutional questions; a very dangerous doctrine indeed, and one which would place us under the despotism of an oligarchy...The Constitution has erected no such single tribunal."

Thomas Jefferson

Mr. Hamilton said that the judicial branch had a *"total incapacity to support its usurpations by force. They were the weakest of the three departments of power and never attack with success either of the other two."*

Alexander Hamilton

"The judiciary of the United States is the subtle corps of sappers and miners constantly working under ground to undermine the foundations of our confederated fabric. They are construing our constitution from a co-ordination of a general and special government to a general and supreme one alone. This will lay all things at their feet..."

Thomas Jefferson

10. The Constitution gives the fifty states the power over those affairs that it prohibits Congress, the President or any judge to control. (Article I Section 8, Amendment X)

"I acknowledge, in the ordinary course of government, that the exposition of the laws and Constitution devolves upon the judicial. But I beg to know upon what principle it can be contended that any one department draws from the Constitution greater powers than another in marking out the limits of the powers of the several departments."

James Madison

The powers not delegated to congress by the Constitution, nor prohibited by it to the states, are reserved to the states respectively, or to the people. What we are about to consider are certainly not delegated to congress, nor are they noticed in the prohibitions to states; they are therefore reserved either to the states or to the people. Their high nature, their necessity to the general security and happiness will be distinctly perceived."

William Rawle

(Mr.Rawle declined to be the nation's first Attorney General)

"From this view of the powers delegated to the federal government, it will clearly appear that those exclusively granted to it have no relation to the domestic economy of the state. The right of property, with all it's train of incidents, except in the case of authors, and inventors, seems to have been left exclusively to the state regulations; and the rights of persons appear to be no further subject to the control of the federal government, than may he necessary to support the dignity and faith of the nation in it's federal or foreign engagements, and obligations;"

St. George Tucker

"And by the sixth article, it is declared, "that this Constitution, and the laws of the United States, which shall be made in pursuance thereof, and the treaties made, or which shall be made, under the authority of the United States, shall be the supreme law of the land; and the judges in every State shall be bound thereby, any thing in the Constitution or law of any State to the contrary notwithstanding... there is no need of any intervention of the State governments, between the Congress and the people, to execute any one power vested in the general government, and that the Constitution and laws of every State are nullified and declared void, so far as they are or shall be inconsistent with this Constitution, or the laws made in pursuance of it, or with treaties made under the authority of the United States. The government, then, so far as it extends, is a complete one, and not a confederation."

Robert Yates

(Mr. Yates was a delegate to the Constitution Convention and a judge on the New York Supreme Court)

11. **When *We the People* of the United States excommunicate God and virtue from our everyday lives our Constitution will only be good for toilet paper. We must return to Godly Christian beliefs and the characteristics of our Founders or we will not survive the onslaught of evil that is embedded in our government at all levels.**

"Those people who will not be governed by God will be ruled by tyrants."

William Penn

(Mr. Penn was the founder of Pennsylvania; his frame of government served as an inspiration for the U.S. Constitution)

"It is when people forget God that tyrants forge their chains."

Patrick Henry

"If a republican government fails to secure public prosperity and happiness, it must be because the citizens neglect the divine commands, and elect bad men to make and administer the laws."

Noah Webster
(1758-1843)

(Mr. Webster was known as the founder of American Education, he published *Webster's Dictionary*)

"We have staked the whole future of American civilization, not on the power of government, far from it. We have staked the future of all our political institutions upon the capacity of mankind of self-government; upon the capacity of each and all of us to govern ourselves, to control ourselves, to sustain ourselves according to the **Ten Commandments of God.**"

James Madison

12. An amendment must be added to the Constitution that only gives the voting right to citizens who either pay some form of federal tax, own property or businesses or have served a minimum of five years in the military with honor. (Article V)

"Our Founding Fathers had no debates on who voted, for only men who owned property voted. Each knew that those who owned property had greater concerns about government legislation and the

character of their politicians than those who had nothing invested in how the Constitution-bound government operated. Thereafter, the voting amendments were added to the Constitution that allow everybody from the age of eighteen and above to vote; this includes the forty-seven percent who do not pay taxes, such as college students, freeloaders, welfare recipients and drug pushers; all who only care for more unconstitutional government handouts and will only vote for the corrupt politicians that will promise greater gratuities."

Bill Basaar

13. **The liberty of the press does not condone the right to defame, affront, falsely accuse, hide the truth or change the story. By these acts of evil, people frame their ideology based on lies and deceit with the sole purpose to have *We the People* agree that the Constitution must be declared null and void. (Amendment I)**

"If by the liberty of the press were understood merely the liberty of discussing the propriety of public measures and political opinions, let us have as much of it as you please: But if it means the liberty of affronting, calumniating and defaming one another, I, for my part, own myself willing to part with my share of it, whenever our legislators shall please so to alter the law and shall cheerfully consent to exchange my liberty of abusing others for the privilege of not being abused myself."

Benjamin Franklin

"What is meant by the liberty of the press is that there should be no antecedent restraint upon it; but that every author is responsible when he attacks the security or welfare of the government, or the safety, character, and property of the individual."

James Wilson
(Mr. Wilson signed the Declaration of Independence and Constitution; original justice of the Supreme Court)

"It seems really as if our newspapers were busy to spread superstition. Omens and dreams, and prodigies are recorded, as if they were worth minding. The increasing fashion for printing wonderful tales of crimes and accidents is worse than ridiculous, as it corrupts both the public taste and morals. It multiplies fables and crimes, and thus makes shocking things familiar while it withdraws popular attention from familiar truth, because it is not shocking. Surely, extraordinary events have not the best title to our studious attention. To study nature or man we ought to know things that are in the ordinary course, not the unaccountable things that happen out of it."

Fisher Ames
(1758-1808)
(Mr. Ames was a Massachusetts congressman)

14. **Property tax of any kind, issued by local, state, or federal governments is immoral and a crime against the people's liberties. Tyranny reigns when the government via their law confiscates our property for payment of these taxes.**

"As a man is said to have a right to his property, he may be equally said to have a property in his rights. Where an excess of power prevails property of no sort is duly respected. No man is safe in his opinions, his person, his faculties, or his possessions."

James Madison

"The moment the idea is admitted into society that property is not as sacred as the laws of God, and that there is not a force of law and public justice to protect it, anarchy and tyranny commence."

John Adams

"Government is instituted to protect property of every sort; as well that which lies in the various rights of individuals, as that which the term particularly expresses. This being the end of government, that alone is a just government which impartially secures to every man whatever is his own."

James Madison

"Direct taxation can go but little way towards raising a revenue. To raise money in this way, people must be provident; they must be constantly laying up money to answer the demands of the collector. But you cannot make people thus provident; if you would do anything to purpose you must come in when they are spending, and take a part with them. This does not take away the tools of a man's business, or the necessary utensils of this family: it only comes in when he is taking his pleasure, and feels generous."

Oliver Ellsworth
(Mr. Ellsworth was one of five men who prepared the first draft of the Constitution)

15. **Congress must pass a balanced budget amendment. If *We the People* allow Congress to operate without a balanced budget, and we do not vote them out of office, we will suffer the oppression and wretchedness that follows.**

> *"I go on this great republican principle, that the people will have virtue and intelligence to select men of virtue and wisdom. Is there no virtue among us? If there be not, we are in a wretched situation. Theoretical checks—no form of government can render us secure. To suppose that any form of government will secure liberty or happiness without virtue in people is a chimerical idea. If there be sufficient virtue and intelligence in the community, it will be exercised in the selection of these men. So that we do not depend on their virtue, or put confidence in the rulers, but in the people who are to choose them."*
>
> James Madison

> *"There is far more danger in public than in private monopoly, for when Government goes into business it can always shift it's loses to the taxpayers. Government never makes ends meet—and that is the first requisite of business."*
>
> Thomas Edison.

16. **A tyrannical government sends us deeper into debt and cares less about balancing our nation's accounts while they take more of *We the People's* tax dollars and borrow more money for their favorite projects as they pad their private accounts. Yet, we elect these same politicians again and again.**

"I predict future happiness for Americans if they can prevent the government from wasting the labors of the people under the pretense of taking care of them."

Thomas Jefferson

"As the cool and deliberate sense of the community ought in all governments, and actually will in all free governments ultimately prevail over the views of its rulers; so there are particular moments in public affairs, when the people stimulated by some irregular passion, or some illicit advantage, or misled by the artful misrepresentations of interested men, may call for measures which they themselves will afterwards be the most ready to lament and condemn. In these critical moments, how salutary will be the interference of some temperate and respectable body of citizens, in order to check the misguided career, and to suspend the blow mediated by the people against themselves, until reason, justice and truth, can regain their authority over the public mind?

James Madison

"To contract new debts is not the way to pay old ones."

George Washington

17. **If it is not enumerated in the Constitution as a Congressional power, it is a State power. If the Federal Government makes unconstitutional laws, the states must nullify the laws. If an elected politician is worthy of their office they will speak out against the tyranny that reigns in our government, and if not, we need to throw them out of office. (Article I Section 8, Amendment X)**

"Congress has not unlimited powers to provide for the general welfare but only those specifically enumerated."

Thomas Jefferson

"The congress of the United States possesses no power to regulate, or interfere with the domestic concerns, or police of any state: it belongs not to them to establish any rules respecting the rights of property;"

St. George Tucker

"The Constitution is not a document for the government to restrain the people: it is an instrument for the people to restrain the government- lest it come to dominate our lives and our interests."

Patrick Henry

"RESOLVED: That the principle and construction contended for by sundry of the state legislatures, that the general government is the exclusive judge of the extent of the powers delegated to it, stop nothing short of despotism; since the discretion of those who administer the government, and not the constitution, would be the measure of their powers: That the several states who formed that instrument, being sovereign and independent, have the unquestionable right to judge of its infraction; and that a nullification, by those sovereignties, of all unauthorized acts done under colour of that instrument, is the rightful remedy."

Thomas Jefferson

18. All lobbyists, all corporate leaders, all officers of unions and all political parties and foreign

governments that lobby or meet any elected politician or congressional staff members or members of the executive branch must have those meetings recorded and made available to *We the People* by way of the internet.

"The liberties of a people never were, nor ever will be, secure, when the transactions of their rulers may be concealed from them."

Patrick Henry

"The right of freely examining public characters and measures, and of free communication among the people thereon...has ever been justly deemed the only effectual guardian of every other right."

James Madison
(December 21, 1798)

"I used to say that politics is the second oldest profession (prostitution being the oldest), but I have come to realize that it bears a gross similarity to the first."

Ronald Reagan

19. **The President, the Judges, and the members of Congress do not provide our nation's families an anxiety, agitation free life, nor do they protect our liberty from government harassment that they swore to give to *We the People of the United States;* these elected tyrants must be removed from office.**

"The time has come that Christians must vote for honest men and take consistent ground in politics or the Lord will curse them… Christians have been exceedingly guilty in this manner. But the time has come when they must act differently…Christians seem to act as if they thought God did not see what they do in politics. But I tell you He does see it—and He will bless or curse this nation according to the course they take."

Charles Finney

(Charles Finney was the leading evangelist of the Second Great Awakening, an avid abolitionist, president of Oberlin College from 1851-1866, a college that accepted Afro-American students)

We the People of the United States, in Order to form a more perfect Union, establish Justice, insure domestic Tranquility, provide for the common defense, promote general Welfare, and secure the Blessings of Liberty to ourselves and our posterity, do ordain and establish this Constitution for the United States of America.

The United States Constitution

"The views of men can only be known, or guessed at, by their words or actions."

George Washington

20. **The President's executive orders that affect those outside the executive branch are Unconstitutional. Article II does not allow the President to dictate these orders. All executive orders issued by any President in our history that created any law or any government department must be rescinded**

immediately by Congress. Executive orders are dictator edicts.
(Article I Section 8, Article II Section 2 & 3)

"They who would give up an essential liberty for temporary security, deserve neither liberty or security."

Benjamin Franklin

"It is sufficiently obvious, that persons and property are the two great subjects on which Governments are to act; and that the rights of persons, and the rights of property, are the objects, for the protection of which Government was instituted. These rights cannot well be separated"

James Madison
(December 2, 1829)

"...by an unconstitutional act of congress...for the purpose of giving to the president powers, which the constitution expressly denied him, and an influence the most dangerous that can be conceived, to the peace, liberty, and happiness of the United States."

St. George Tucker

"Patriotism is the last refuge of scoundrels"
William Samuel Johnson

21. Our Constitutional freedoms are dying from the tyranny of over 100,000 new laws and more than 160,000 pages of regulation that have placed a

stranglehold on our freedoms over recent years. They must be rescinded.
(Article I Section 8, Amendment X)

"The more laws, the less justice."

Marcus Cicero
(Mr. Cicero was a Roman philosopher, orator, political theorist & constitutionalist)

"Congress has not unlimited powers to provide for the general welfare but only those specifically enumerated."

Thomas Jefferson

22. Not one branch of the Federal Government, not one Executive Cabinet Department, not even the Justice Department, has any Constitutional Authority to dictate or sue any state on any grounds, except when the people's Constitutional rights have been violated.
(Article I Section 8, Article VI, Amendment X)

"The powers delegated by the proposed Constitution to the federal government are few and defined. Those which are to remain in the State governments are numerous and indefinite."

James Madison
(January 26, 1788)

"On every question of construction, let us carry ourselves back to the time when the Constitution was adopted, recollect the spirit manifested in the debates, and instead of trying what meaning may be squeezed out of the text, or invented against it, conform to the probable one in which it was passed."

Thomas Jefferson

23. **The Constitution allows only Congress to create laws and regulations in eighteen specified areas. If the President enacts an executive order, appoints judges with no regard for the Constitution or his Justice Department decides not to follow bankruptcy or voter laws, Congress must impeach him.**
(Article I Section 8, Article II Section 2 & 3)

"The powers delegated by the proposed Constitution to the federal government are few and defined. Those which are to remain in the State governments are numerous and indefinite."

James Madison

"No political truth is certainly of greater intrinsic value, or is stamped with the authority of more enlightened patrons of liberty than that on which the objection is founded. The accumulation of all powers, legislative, executive, and judiciary, in the same hands, whether of one, a few, or many, and whether hereditary, self-appointed, or elective, may justly be pronounced the very definition of tyranny."

James Madison

24. **It is tyranny when our government takes the people's money to aid enemy governments, foreign politicians and despicable organizations.**

> *"To compel a man to subsidize with his taxes the propagation of ideas which he disbelieves and abhors is sinful and tyrannical."*
>
> Thomas Jefferson

> *"Foreign aid is taxing poor people in rich countries for the benefit of rich people in poor countries."*
>
> Bernard Rosenberg
>
> (Mr. Rosenberg was Professor at City University of New York. He wrote, *Dictionary for the Disenchanted*, 1972)

25. **The redistribution of wealth amongst the nation's people is clearly unconstitutional.**
    (Article I Section 8)

> *"The utopian schemes of leveling and redistribution of wealth are arbitrary, despotic, and in our government unconstitutional."*
>
> Samuel Adams

> *"The office of government is not to confer happiness, but to give men the opportunity to work out happiness for themselves."*
>
> William Ellery
>
> (Mr. Ellery signed The Declaration of Independence)

26. **Any form of income tax is tyrannical, hence unconstitutional. We must repeal the Sixteenth Amendment of the Constitution. When the IRS can seize your personal property, confiscate your money or harass with penalties that could send you to jail, the Constitutional right to own property without the government's intervention has been destroyed.**

    "The power to tax involves the power to destroy."

    John Marshall

    (Mr. Marshall was the fourth Chief Justice of the United States)

    "Taxes on consumption are always least burdensome, because they are least felt, and are borne too by those who are both willing and able to pay them; that of all taxes on consumption, those on foreign commerce are most compatible with the genius and policy of free states."

    James Madison

27. **By what Article in the Constitution or Amendment does our federal government have the right to monitor and seize our bank accounts? This is absolute tyranny! This is absolutely unconstitutional!**
    (Article I Section 8 does not give our government this power)

"The Constitution is not an instrument for the government to restrain the people, it is an instrument for the people to restrain the government—lest it come to dominate our lives and interests."

Patrick Henry

"Necessity is the plea for every infringement of human freedom. It is the argument of tyrants. It is the creed of slaves."

William Pitt the younger
(1759-1806)
(British Prime Minister who argued for peace with America)

"Government is instituted to protect property of every sort; as well that which lies in the various rights of individuals, as that which the term particularly expresses. This being the end of government, that alone is a just government which impartially secures to every man whatever is his own."

James Madison

28. **The FBI operations that take authority over local police forces are unconstitutional and must be stopped by Congress. The FBI was created with an executive order, which is also unconstitutional. (Article I Section 8, Article II Section 2 & 3)**

"The congress of the United States possesses no power to regulate, or interfere with the domestic concerns, or police of any state: it belongs not to them to establish any rules respecting the rights of property; nor will the constitution permit any prohibition of arms to the people;"

St. George Tucker

"The first and governing maxim in the interpretation of a statute is to discover the meaning of those who made it."

James Wilson

(Mr. Wilson signed the Constitution and was an original justice of the Supreme Court)

29. Our employees, all Congress members, who refuse to fulfill their Constitutional duties, must be fired by *We the people*. It is by Constitutional authority that they order all executive orders to cease.
(No Article, Section or Amendment allows executive orders)

"We the people are the rightful masters of both Congress and the Courts—not to overthrow the Constitution, but to overthrow the men who pervert the Constitution."

Abraham Lincoln

"When injustice becomes law, resistance becomes duty."

Thomas Jefferson

"In framing a government which is to be administered by men over men, the great difficulty lies in this: you must first enable the government to control the governed: and in the next place, oblige it to control itself."

James Madison

30. Narrow is the way that secures our liberties within the exact meaning of the words in the

Constitution and broad is the way to tyranny when the Constitution is interpreted to meet social or political ideology.

"On every question of construction, let us carry ourselves back to the time when the Constitution was adopted, recollect the spirit manifested in the debates, and instead of trying what meaning may be squeezed out of the text, or invented against it, conform to the probable one in which it was passed."

Thomas Jefferson

"If Congress can do whatever in their discretion can be done by money, and will promote the General Welfare, the Government is no longer a limited one, possessing enumerated powers, but an indefinite one, subject to particular exceptions."

James Madison

31. It is tyranny when Congress gives the President sole authority to seize farms, businesses, whole towns or any private property, when he or she can on a whim determine that the country is in a state of emergency; EO# 13575.
(Article I Section 8, Article II Section 2 & 3 do not permit these orders)

"The greatest (calamity) which could befall (us would be) submission to a government of unlimited powers."

Thomas Jefferson

"The greater the power, the more dangerous the abuse."

Edmund Burke
(Mr. Burke was a member of the British Parliament, devoted to liberty and American Independence)

"When all government, domestic and foreign, in little as in great things, shall be drawn to Washington as the center of all power, it will render powerless the checks provided of one government on another, and will become as venal and oppressive as the government from which we separated."

Thomas Jefferson

32. **It is tyranny in operation when Republican and Democrat politicians place extreme limits on debate. In every venue of society we allow our leaders and politicians to limit political debate by merely having a question and answer format on every important issue.**

"Freedom of discussion, unaided by power, is...sufficient for the propagation and protection of truth."

Thomas Jefferson

"A single seemingly powerless person who dares to cry out the word of truth and to stand behind it with all his person and all his life has surprisingly, greater power, though formally disenfranchised, than do thousands of anonymous voters."

Vaclav Havel
(Mr. Havel was a playwright, a dissident against the Soviet Union invasion; later he became the Czech Republic President from 1993-2003).

33. Dodd-Frank and Sarbanes-Oxley legislation must be repealed immediately.
(Article I Section 8 does not give Congress the authority to regulate businesses)

"A wise and frugal government, which shall restrain men from injuring one another, which shall leave them otherwise free to regulate their own pursuits of industry and improvement, and shall not take from the mouth of labor the bread it has earned. This is the sum of good government, and this is necessary to close the circle of our felicity."

Thomas Jefferson
(First Inaugural Address)

34. When *We the People* remain silent, when business men say nothing for the fear of losing money, when our political leaders dare not speak the truth about our government's tyrannical laws because of their fear of the media and opposition rhetoric, their silence makes them complicit and accountable for the government ruling by fiat over the country.

"My reading of history convinces me that most bad government results from too much government."

Thomas Jefferson

"For true patriots to be silent, is dangerous."

Samuel Adams

"All tyranny needs to gain a foothold is for people of good conscience to remain silent."

Thomas Jefferson

'Nip the shoots of arbitrary power in the bud, is the only maxim which can ever preserve the liberties of any people."

John Adams

35. **We must have a whirlwind of long passionate debates that denounce the crimes of the Constitutional imposters. We need to startle and quicken the people into action who then vote all the imposters out of political office.**

"I go on this great republican principle, that the people will have virtue and intelligence to select men of virtue and wisdom. Is there no virtue among us? If there be not, we are in a wretched situation. Theoretical checks—no form of government can render us secure. To suppose that any form of government will secure liberty or happiness without virtue in people is a chimerical idea. If there be sufficient virtue and intelligence in the community, it will be exercised in the selection of these men. So that we do not depend on their virtue, or put confidence in the rulers, but in the people who are to choose them."

James Madison

"It is not light that is needed, but fire; it is not the gentle shower, but thunder. We need the storm, the whirlwind and the earthquake. The feeling of the nation must be quickened; the conscience of the nation

must be roused; the propriety of the nation must be startled; the hypocrisy of the nation must be exposed; its crimes against God and man must be proclaimed and denounced."

Frederick Douglass

(1818-1895)

(Mr. Douglass was a slave who freed himself; an orator, an abolitionist, a black man for women's suffrage, an advisor of many U.S. Presidents)

36. **Political party platforms are merely worthless words. We presume they mean something when they are just a pretense of the politicians doing something that wastes the good intentioned efforts of convention delegates.**

"If ever time should come, when vain and aspiring men shall possess the highest seats in Government, our country will stand in need of its experienced patriots to prevent its ruin."

Samuel Adams

"The views of men can only be known, or guessed at, by their words or actions."

George Washington

"When the righteous rule, the people rejoice; when the wicked rule, the people groan."

William Patterson

(Supreme Court Justice reminding his fellow justices in 1800)

37. **If Congressional members cannot manage the Constitutional laws it passes, then Congress must turn that issue over to the states. No unelected lawyer or other underlings of any bureaucracy must be allowed to dictate what the passed bill legally says. (Article I Section 8, Amendment X)**

> *"The essence of government is power; and power, lodged as it must be in human hands, will ever be liable to abuse."*
>
> James Madison

38. **It should be illegal and punished as a federal crime when any rule or regulation is written into any government legislation and passed into law without the full knowledge of *We the People.* (Congress has the power to make laws ONLY in the areas listed in Article I Section 8!)**

> *"The liberties of a people never were, nor ever will be, secure, when the transactions of their rulers may be concealed from them."*
>
> Patrick Henry

> *"If the federal government should overpass the just bounds of its authority and make a tyrannical use of its powers, the people, whose creature it is, must appeal to the standard they have formed, and take such measures to redress the injury done to the Constitution as the exigency may suggest and prudence justify."*
>
> Alexander Hamilton

39. When Godless judges order from their tyrannical, evil ideology that any form of Christianity must be eliminated from the public square, they are tyrants who must be removed from the bench.
(The First Amendment orders that the government shall make NO LAW PROHIBITING the free exercise of religion)

"Finally, let us not forget the religious character of our origin. Our fathers were brought hither by their high veneration for the Christian religion. They journeyed by its light, and labored in its hope. They sought to incorporate its principles with the elements of their society, and to diffuse its influence through all their institutions, civil, political, or literary."

Daniel Webster

(1782-1852)

(Mr. Webster was a Constitutional lawyer, Secretary of State under three presidents)

"The real object of the First Amendment was not to coutenance, much less to advance Mohammedanism, Judaism, or infidelity, by prostrating Christianity, but to exculde all rivalry among Christian sects and to prevent any national ecclesiastical patronage of the national government."

Joseph Story

(Mr. Story was appointed to the Supreme Court by James Madison)

"Whoever is an avowed enemy of God, I scruple not to call him an enemy of his country."

John Witherspoon

(Mr. Witherspoon signed the Declaration of Independence)

40. **The Bible must be the major textbook in all schools. If a power is not enumerated in the Constitution, it is a power delegated to the states. (Article I Section 8, Amendment I & X)**

"Education is worthless without the Bible."

Noah Webster

"Religion is the only solid basis of good morals; therefore education should teach the precepts of religion and the duties of man toward God."

Gouverneur Morris

(Mr. Morris represented Pennsylvania at the Constitutional Convention; known as the 'Penman of the Constitution')

"The teachings of the Bible are so interwoven and entwined with our whole civic and social life that it would be literally...impossible for us to figure what that loss would be if these teachings were removed. We would lose almost all the standards by which we now judge both public and private morals; all the standards towards which we, with more or less resolution, strive to raise ourselves."

Theodore Roosevelt

"In the name of God...in the name of truth...teaching about religion must be demanded and provided for the children of today, if this democracy and this civilization are to survive."

Peter Marshall
(Mr. Marshall was a Presbyterian minister. He served as U.S. Senate Chaplain for two years from 1947-1949)

41. The education of our children is the sole responsibility of first the parents, second the local people, then the state. Education is not enumerated in the Constitution; therefore, it is a state power. (Article I Section 8, Amendment X)

"In my view, the Christian religion is the most important and one of the first things in which all children, under a free government ought to be instructed....No truth is more evident to my mind than that the Christian religion must be the basis of any government intended to secure the rights and privileges of a free people."

Noah Webster

"If it is important for us to teach our children the laws that govern safe driving, is it not also important to teach them the laws that govern safe living? The moral law has this function—to teach us how to live safely in a moral world."

John R. Richardson
(In *Christian Economics,* Mr. Richardson wrote, *"The Christian Message to the Market Place,"* published in 1966 by St. Thomas Press, Houston)

42. **Marriage is only between a man and a woman. This has always been a church responsibility. This issue is not enumerated in the Constitution; therefore, it is not a federal government power. (Article I Section 8, Amendment I & X)**

"The foundation of national morality must be laid in private families...How is it possible that Children can have any just sense of the sacred Obligations of Morality or Religion if, from their earliest Infancy, they learn their Mothers live in habitual Infidelity to their fathers, and their fathers in as constant Infidelity to their Mothers?"

John Adams

"How strangely will the Tools of a Tyrant pervert the plain Meaning of Words!"

Samuel Adams

"Woe to those who call evil good and good evil; who put darkness for light and light for darkness; who put bitter for sweet and sweet for bitter! Woe to those who are wise in their own eyes and prudent in their own sight!"

The Bible
(Isaiah 5:20-21)

43. **The people shall be given an agreed to length of time to read any document proposed to be made law. When Congress conceals its legislation from the people in any way, shape or form, they are a deceitful and untrustworthy body equivalent to the 7 things that God hates the most.**

(The meanings of the Hebrew text are included in brackets) *These six things does the Lord hate: yes, seven are an abomination to him: a proud look, a lying tongue...A false witness that speaks lies...*(The truth will only be told if it is to their advantage, otherwise the evil person will lie. A false witness premeditates lies then concocts lying schemes in order to carry out a deceitful evil plan.) *vs.17- and hands that shed innocent blood.* (This pertains to murderers; however it also pertains to those who murder one's character.)

The Bible
(Proverbs 6:16-19)

44. **Any form of deceitful or intended dissension created by a political figure or media person that stirs up raucous disagreements amongst *We the People* for the purpose of getting votes or favors from companies or other politicians are the evils that God hates the most.**

...The Lord hates he who sows discord among the people. (Any politician, who demeans, smears, lies, deceives or sows dissension amongst the country's citizens for the purpose of carrying out political schemes is an evil person. Politicians causing racial hate and inciting the poor against the rich are good examples.)

The Bible
(Proverbs 6:19)

"Be not intimidated...nor suffer yourselves to be wheedled out of your liberties by any pretense of politeness, delicacy, or decency. These, as they are often used, are but three different names for hypocrisy, chicanery and cowardice."

John Adams

45. **It is evil and illegal when a leader intends to harm any selected group of people or any religion or any cause that is not promoting his or her ideals. Freedom of speech does not grant any one religion a favorable speech status, or another an unfavorable status.**
(Amendment I)

"It cannot be emphasized too strongly or too often that this great nation was founded, not by religionists, but by Christians: not on religions, but on the gospel of Jesus Christ! For this very reason peoples of other faiths have been afforded asylum, prosperity, and freedom of worship here."

Patrick Henry

"For avoiding the extremes of despotism or anarchy...the only ground of hope must be on the morals of the people. I believe that religion is the only solid base of morals and that morals are the only possible support of free governments."

Gouverneur Morris

"Everyone who takes delight in publicly or privately taking away any person's good name, or striving to render him ridiculous, are in the fall

of bitterness, and in the bonds of iniquity, whatever their presences may be for it."

Sarah Updike Goddard
(1700-1770)
(Sarah was the 2nd woman publisher in Rhode Island)

46. The Constitution gives the Federal Government the responsibility in only two areas: economic protection from corrupt corporations and dishonest people, and safety from foreign armies and insurrections. (Preamble, Article I Section 8, allows the regulation of commerce between states and the authority over bankruptcies and counterfeiting)

"Government is instituted for the common good; for the protection, safety, prosperity and happiness of the people; and not for profit, honor, or private interest of any one man, family, or class of men; therefore, the people alone have an incontestable, unalienable and indefeasible right to institute government; and to reform, alter or totally change the same, when their protection, safety, prosperity and happiness require it."

John Adams

"RESOLVED: That the principle and construction contended for by sundry of the state legislatures, that the general government is the exclusive judge of the extent of the powers delegated to it, stop nothing short of despotism; since the discretion of those who administer the government, and not the constitution, would be the measure of their powers: That the several states who formed that instrument, being

sovereign and independent, have the unquestionable right to judge of its infraction; and that a nullification, by those sovereignties, of all unauthorized acts done under colour of that instrument, is the rightful remedy."

Thomas Jefferson

47. **The State Governments alone are responsible for their people's civil rights, their recovery from natural disasters, their laws and police affairs, for their fish and wildlife, their agricultural and other operations or issues that concern their state, its counties, cities and towns. Again, as noted before, if it is not written in the Constitution as a power for Congress, it is a state issue!**
(Article I Section 8, Amendment X)

"The way to have safe government is not to trust it all to the one, but to divide it among the many, distributing to everyone exactly the functions in which he is competent…to let the National Government be entrusted with the defense of the nation, and its foreign and federal relations…the State Governments with the Civil Rights, laws, Police and administration of what concerns the State generally. The Counties with local concerns and each ward direct the interests within itself. It is by dividing and subdividing these Republics from the great national down… Until it ends in the administration of everyman's farm by himself…that all will be done for the best."

Thomas Jefferson

48. **It is criminal for any government to take taxes and pay for abortions and birth control through grants**

to institutions that donate some of that money to those politicians who made it possible to receive the government money legally stolen from *We the People.* The abortion issue is strictly a state power! (Article I Section 8, Amendment X)

"Human law must rest its authority ultimately upon the authority of that law which is divine...Far from being rivals or enemies, religion and law are twin sisters, friends, and mutual assistants. Indeed, these two sciences run into each other."

James Wilson

(Mr. Wilson spoke 168 times at the Constitution Convention)

"No matter how noble the objectives of government, if it blurs decency and kindness, cheapens life and breeds ill-will and suspicion, it is an evil government."

Eric Hoffer

(1902-1983)

(Mr. Hoffer was an American moral & social philosopher)

49. The Supreme Court ruled that the mandated insurance in the ObamaCare legislation was a tax, even though it wasn't a tax. This is taxation without representation and *We the People* must force Congress to overrule the arbitrary Supreme Court.
(Article I Section 8, Amendment X)

"Were the power of judging joined with the legislature, the life and liberty of the subject would be exposed to arbitrary control, for the judge would then be the legislator. Were it joined to executive power, the judge might behave with the violence of the oppressor."

James Madison

"And it proves, in the last place, that liberty can have nothing to fear from the judiciary alone, but would have everything to fear from its union with either of the other departments."

Alexander Hamilton

50. Our courts are to use only the U.S Constitution as the basis of any ruling. If they use any other document for their ruling, that judge, or judges, must be impeached by Congress and removed from their seat on that court.
(Article III Section 2, Article VI)

"As a member of this court I am not justified in writing any private notions into the Constitution, no matter how deeply I may cherish them or how mischievous I may deem their disregard."

Felix Frankfurter
(Mr. Frankfurter served on the U.S. Supreme Court from 1939-1962)

"When they (the judges) consider its (a law's) principles and find it to be incompatible with the superior power of the Constitution, it is their duty to pronounce it void."

James Wilson

51. All Court rulings must be based on the facts of that case and not on previous court cases. A precedent ruling should not apply to any other case.

"There can never be danger that the judges, by a series of deliberate usurpations on the authority of the legislature would hazard the united resentment of the body entrusted with it, while this body was possessed of the means of punishing their presumption by degrading them from their stations."

Alexander Hamilton

"I acknowledge, in the ordinary course of government, that the exposition of the laws and Constitution devolves upon the judicial. But I beg to know upon what principle it can be contended that any one department draws from the Constitution greater powers than another in marking out the limits of the powers of the several departments.

James Madison

52. Only blind justice is Constitutional, not social justice.

"The worst tyranny is that of misapplied laws."

Klemens Metternich
(1773-1859)
(Mr. Metternich was a German politician, statesman & diplomat)

"The great desideratum in Government is, so to modify the sovereignty as that it may be sufficiently neutral between different parts of the

Society to control one part from invading the rights of another, and at the same time sufficiently controlled itself, from setting up an interest adverse to that of the entire Society."

James Madison
(October 24, 1787)

"The judges must interpret the laws; they ought not to be legislators."
Rufus King
(Mr. King signed the Constitution; he was also a U.S. senator who helped frame The Bill of Rights)

53. **Any Judge must be replaced if they believe that any court ruling alone shall be the law of the land, be it one judge or a panel of judges. Judicial supremacy is not constitutional.**
(Article III Section 2)

Alexander Hamilton argued for modifications to the judiciary. *"The national legislature will have ample authority to make such exceptions, and to prescribe such regulations as will be calculated to obviate or remove these inconveniences."*

Alexander Hamilton

"You seem...to consider the judges as the ultimate arbiters of all constitutional questions; a very dangerous doctrine indeed, and one which would place us under the despotism of an oligarchy...the Constitution has erected no such single tribunal."

Thomas Jefferson

54. The Constitution gives the Federal Government one main duty; protect *We the People* from foreign powers that desire to harm us by any means. If our energy supply is subject to unreliable foreign governments, then *We the People* are at the mercy of our tyrant President and the tyrants in Congress. (Preamble, Article I Section 8)

"The diversity in the faculties of men from which the rights of property originate, is not less an insuperable obstacle to a uniformity of interests. The protection of these faculties is the first object of government."

James Madison

"The great rule of conduct for us in regard to foreign nations is, in extending our commercial relations to have with them as little political connection as possible. ...Why, by interweaving our destiny with that of any part of Europe, entangle our peace and prosperity in the toils of European ambition, rivalship, interest, humor, or caprice? It is our true policy to steer clear of permanent alliances with any portion of the foreign world. ...We may safely trust to temporary alliances for extraordinary emergencies. ...There can be no greater error than to expect or calculate upon real favors from nation to nation. It is an illusion which experience must cure, which a just pride ought to discard."

George Washington

"...know how deeply I am impressed with a sense of the importance of Amendments; that the good people may clearly see the distinction,

for there is a distinction, between the federal powers vested in Congress and the sovereign authority belonging to the several States, which is the Palladium (the protection) of the private and personal rights of the citizens."

Samuel Adams

55. Congress, not the President, must provide for our protection and give our country's businesses the ability to attain all our natural energy resources. Oil, coal, natural gas, new refineries, pipe lines, wind and solar sources shall be under the power of each state.
(Article I Section 8, Amendment X)

"Government is instituted to protect property of every sort; as well that which lies in the various rights of individuals, as that which the term particularly expresses. This being the end of government, that alone is a just government which impartially secures to every man whatever is his own."

James Madison

56. If the tyrannical members in Congress will not rescind the thousands of regulations that hinder the building of new refineries nor allow exploration for oil and gas nor allow drilling and mining anywhere, they must be removed from office for negligence of their Constitutional duty.

"In framing a government which is to be administered by men over men the great difficulty lies in this: You must first enable the government to control the governed, and in the next place, oblige it to control itself"
James Madison

57. **Our borders must be controlled from the onslaught of foreigners that come into our country illegally, and if not completely stopped by Congress; their lack of concern for our safety from terrorists is comparable to treason.**
(Article I Section 8 grants Congress the power of naturalization rules.)

"Some reasonable term ought to be allowed to enable aliens to get rid of foreign and acquire American attachments; to learn the principles and imbibe the spirit of our government; and to admit of a probability at least, of their feeling a real interest in our affairs."
Alexander Hamilton

58. **Illegal aliens have no U.S. Constitutional rights; they have broken our laws and must be deported. Therefore, they must receive no schooling, no social security, no free healthcare and no license of any kind.**
(Article I Section 8 grants Congress ONLY <u>eighteen</u> areas of power over its own citizens; these areas of power are not included in the provisions above and certainly must not be provided to illegals)

"The great desideratum in Government is, so to modify the sovereignty as that it may be sufficiently neutral between different parts of the Society to control one part from invading the rights of another, and at the same time sufficiently controlled itself, from setting up an interest adverse to that of the entire Society."

James Madison
(October 24, 1787)

59. **Congress must pass a mandatory moratorium on Congress and all federal government departments that they must not issue any new regulation or law until one-half of those created in the last fifteen years are rescinded.**

"In the first place, it is to be remembered, that the general government is not to be charged with the whole power of making and administering laws: its jurisdiction is limited to certain enumerated objects, which concern all the members of the republic, but which are not to be attained by the separate provisions of any."

James Madison
(November 30, 1787)

60. **Since the 1950's all the new laws and new regulations ordered by the Presidents, the executive operated offices or by bureaucratic agencies are unconstitutional. In the guise of help, our liberties and money are taken from *We the People* that causes even greater economic distress.**

"If Congress can do whatever in their discretion can be done by money, and will promote the General Welfare, the Government is no longer a limited one, possessing enumerated powers, but an indefinite one, subject to particular exceptions."

James Madison
(January 21, 1792)

61. **Life before 1950 brought us more freedom and happiness when many of us worked happily for businesses that were barely regulated. Most of us still live happily in houses, on property built before all the government regulations.**

"A successful economy depends on the proliferation of the rich, on creating a large class of risk-taking men who are willing to shun the easy channels of a comfortable life in order to create new enterprise, win huge profits, and invest them again."

George Gilder
(1939-)
(Mr. Gilder has authored many economic books)

62. **Government is to protect life, not inject death. Life is our unalienable right given by God. Death inflicted on the unborn by Judges is murder. This is tyranny and it is evil; the Constitution does not allow Judges to make laws.**

"To compel a man to subsidize with his taxes the propagation of ideas which he disbelieves and abhors is sinful and tyrannical."

Thomas Jefferson

"We hold these truths to be self-evident, that all men are created equal, that they are endowed by their Creator with certain unalienable Rights, that among these are Life, Liberty and the pursuit of Happiness. That to secure these rights, Governments are instituted among Men, deriving their just powers from the consent of the governed, —That whenever any Form of Government becomes destructive of these ends, it is the Right of the People to alter or to abolish it, and to institute new Government, laying its foundation on such principles and organizing its powers in such form, as to them shall seem most likely to effect their safety and Happiness."

The Declaration of Independence

63. An immoral people elect ungodly, immoral politicians who will assume total authority. Career politicians translate into bigger tyrannical governments in towns, cities, counties, states and at the federal level.

"If we abide by the principles taught in the Bible, our country will go on prospering and to prosper; but if we and our posterity neglect its instructions and authority, no man can tell how sudden a catastrophe may overwhelm us and bury all our glory in profound obscurity."

Daniel Webster

"Religion is the only solid basis of good morals; therefore education should teach the precepts of religion and the duties of man toward God."
Gouverneur Morris

"I go on this great republican principle, that the people will have virtue and intelligence to select men of virtue and wisdom. Is there no virtue among us? If there be not, we are in a wretched situation. Theoretical checks—no form of government can render us secure. To suppose that any form of government will secure liberty or happiness without virtue in people is a chimerical idea. If there be sufficient virtue and intelligence in the community, it will be exercised in the selection of these men. So that we do not depend on their virtue, or put confidence in the rulers, but in the people who are to choose them."
James Madison

64. **Amendment XVII must be rescinded and the election of senators returned to the way our Founding Fathers knew was better for state representation and with less chance for a Senator to remain in office till they die. We also need different local business people of strong moral character elected into the House of Representatives every two to four years; career politicians translate into more tyrants.**

"Neither the wisest constitution nor the wisest laws will secure the liberty and happiness of a people whose manners are universally corrupt. He therefore is the truest friend to the liberty of his country who tries most to promote its virtue, and who...will not suffer a man

to be chosen into any office of power and trust who is not a wise and virtuous man."

Samuel Adams

"I doubt...whether any other Convention...may be able to make a better constitution; for, when you assemble a number of men, to have the advantage of their joint wisdom, you inevitably assemble with those men all their prejudices, their passions, their errors of opinion, their local interests, and their selfish views. From such an assembly can a perfect production be expected? It therefore astonishes me, Sir, to find this system approaching so near to perfection..."

Benjamin Franklin

65. Bartered deals between members of Congress or brokered transactions between said Congressional members and the Executive Branch for any legislation is immoral and this nation governed without morals will be a republic on the endangered species list.

"Governments, like clocks, go from the motion men give them; and as governments are made and moved by men, so by them they are ruined too. Wherefore governments rather depend upon men than men upon governments. Let men be good and the government cannot be bad...But if men be bad, let the government be never so good, they will endeavor to warp and spoil it to their turn...though good laws do well, good men do better; for good laws may want good men and be abolished or invaded by ill men; but good men will never want good laws nor suffer ill ones."

William Penn

66. No animal, bird, fish, insect or reptile of any kind should take priority over the economic livelihood of *We the People.* Congress must protect the people's property rights from the green earth, diehard environmentalist who desires to destroy our American way of life that the Constitution protects.

> *"The diversity in the faculties of men from which the rights of property originate, is not less an insuperable obstacle to a uniformity of interests . The protection of these faculties is the first object of government."*
>
> James Madison
> (November 23, 1787)

67. The Constitution says that the United States can ONLY go to war if first declared by Congress. (Article I Section 8)

> *"On every question of construction let us carry ourselves back to the time when the Constitution was adopted, recollect the spirit manifested in the debates, and instead of trying what meaning may be squeezed out of the text, or invented against it, conform to the probable one in which it was passed."*
>
> Thomas Jefferson

68. The National Defense Act signed into law on Dec. 31, 2011, must be obliterated; this Act authorizes the President dictatorial powers to seize and control everything in the country; no such executive power is listed in Article II Section 2 & 3 of the Constitution.

"The whole of the Bill (of Rights) is a declaration of the right of the people at large or considered as individuals...It establishes some rights of the individual as unalienable and which consequently, no majority has a right to deprive them of."

Albert Gallatin
(Mr. Gallatin was Secretary of Treasury under Jefferson and Madison)

"The congress of the United States possesses no power to regulate, or interfere with the domestic concerns, or police of any state: It belongs not to them to establish any rules respecting the rights of property; nor will the Constitution permit any prohibition of arms to the people;…"

St. George Tucker

69. TSA must be abolished. The Homeland Security Department's powers must be eliminated. Listening to our phones, monitoring search engines and observing everything we do in our daily lives, violates our Fourth Amendment right of privacy.

The right of the people to be secure in their persons, houses, papers, and effects, against unreasonable searches and seizures, shall not be violated, and no warrants shall issue, but upon probable cause, supported by oath or affirmation, and particularly describing the place to be searched, and the persons or things to be seized.

Amendment IV

"They who would give up an essential liberty for temporary security, deserve neither liberty or security."

Benjamin Franklin

"When the people fear their government, there is tyranny; when the government fears the people, there is liberty."

Thomas Jefferson

"The people never give up their liberties but under some delusion."

Edmund Burke

(Mr. Burke was a member of the British Parliament, devoted to liberty and American Independence)

70. Our Fourth Amendment right of privacy has been invaded illegally at our border crossings where U.S. citizen's vehicles and other property are searched without reason or warrants.

"Necessity is the plea for every infringement of human freedom. It is the argument of tyrants. It is the creed of slaves."

William Pitt the younger

"There are men in all ages who mean to govern well, but they mean to govern. They promise to be good masters, but they mean to be masters."

Noah Webster

71. All authorities of all cities, counties, states and federal level must cease their seizures and

searches of fisherman's boats or anyone's boats with no search warrants. It is a violation of the Fourth Amendment! This is tyranny!

"The invasion of private rights is chiefly to be apprehended, not from acts of Government contrary to the sense of its constituents, but from acts in which the Government is the mere instrument of the major number of the Constituents."

James Madison

72. **When our local, state and federal governments make it illegal for you to cut trees or move dirt on your own property and they order extensive tests and expensive procedures before you can build, these are the rules of tyrants.**
    (Amendment IV)

"There is danger from all men. The only maxim of a free government ought to be to trust no man living with the power to endanger the public liberty."

John Adams

73. **Congress must declare Sustainable Development (otherwise known as Agenda 21) illegal and order every county, city and state to rescind every agreement with that organization that will soon control all aspects of our daily lives using their unknown regulations that take control of all properties without any notice to the property owners.**

"It is with government as with medicine. Its only business is the choice of evils. Every law is an evil, for every law is an infraction of liberty."

Jeremy Bentham
(1748-1832)

(Mr. Bentham was a British philosopher, jurist & social reformer)

"For avoiding the extremes of despotism or anarchy...the only ground of hope must be on the morals of the people. I believe that religion is the only solid base of morals and that morals are the only possible support of free governments."

Gouverneur Morris

74. **The Constitution only allows the government to own land that it needs to protect the country. Therefore, Congress must return to the states all the national parks and wilderness areas that it took from the states and if any were bought, they must sell these areas back to the states or to U.S. citizens or U.S. owned and operated companies in the U.S. and use the monies to pay down the government debt.**
(Article I Section 8)

"On every question of construction [of the Constitution] let us carry ourselves back to the time when the Constitution was adopted, recollect the spirit manifested in the debates, and instead of trying what meaning may be squeezed out of the text, or invented against it, conform to the probable one in which it was passed."

Thomas Jefferson
(1823)

"Land is the basis of all wealth."

Adam Smith
(1723-1790)
(Moral philosopher & pioneer of political economics)

"If the federal government should overpass the just bounds of its authority and make a tyrannical use of its powers, the people, whose creature it is, must appeal to the standard they have formed, and take such measures to redress the injury done to the Constitution as the exigency may suggest and prudence justify."

Alexander Hamilton

75. **The powers vested in the Federal Ecology and Energy Departments must be dissolved.**
(Article II Section 2, Amendment X)

76. **The EPA was created by an executive order and must be dissolved.**

"I am more and more convinced that man is a dangerous creature and that power, whether vested in many or a few, is ever grasping, and like the grave cries, "Give, Give."

Abigail Adams

77. **The powers vested in the Federal Fish and Wildlife Department must be dissolved.**
(Article II Section 2, Amendment X)

"(The purpose of a written constitution is) to bind up the several branches of government by certain laws, which, when they transgress, their acts shall become nullities; to render unnecessary an appeal to the people, or in other words a rebellion, on every infraction of their rights, on the peril that their acquiescence shall be construed into an intention to surrender those rights."

Thomas Jefferson

78. **All the powers given to the Agriculture Department must be dissolved.**
    (Article I Section 8, Article II Section 2 & 3, Amendment X)

79. **The President's Czars do not have any authority to rule on any matter nor the authority to enforce any rule.**
    (Article I Section 8, Article II Section 2 & 3)

80. **The Department of Education must be dissolved. Education is the responsibility of the parents at the local and state level.**
    (Article I Section 8, Amendment X)

"Every State has a natural right in cases not within the compact (casus non faederis) to nullify of their own authority all assumptions of power by others within their limits. Without this right, they would be under the dominion, absolute and unlimited, of whosoever might exercise this right of judgment for them."

Thomas Jefferson

81. **The unregulated Federal Reserve must be dissolved and the U.S must go back to a gold standard.**
(Article I Section 8)

> *"The end of democracy and the defeat of the American Revolution will occur when the government falls into the hands of lending institutions and moneyed incorporations."*
>
> Thomas Jefferson

82. **The President's power vested in FEMA is unconstitutional and this dictator-like entity created by executive order 12148 must be dissolved.**

> *"'Useful' and 'necessity' was always the tyrants plea."*
>
> C.S. Lewis
>
> (Mr. Lewis wrote *The Screwtape Letters*, as well as *The Chronicles of Narnia*)

83. **Congress must follow the Constitution and therefore, coin money and regulate the value thereof with the states having the right to pay with gold or silver coins.**
(Article I Section 8 & 10)

> *"If in the opinion of the people the distribution or modification of the constitutional powers be in any particular wrong, let it be corrected by an amendment in the way which the Constitution designates, but let there be no change by usurpation; for though this in one instance may*

be the instrument of good, it is the customary weapon by which free governments are destroyed."

George Washington

84. **Labor unions and public service unions must not be catered to with laws and regulations that favor their members over the private sector businesses and their employees.**

85. **Subsidies contingent on agricultural businesses not growing a certain crop or not raising certain animals must be abolished.**

"If ye love wealth greater than liberty, the tranquility of servitude greater than the animating contest for freedom, go home from us in peace. We seek not your counsel, nor your arms. Crouch down and lick the hand that feeds you; and may posterity forget that ye were our countrymen."

Samuel Adams

86. **It is unconstitutional for the federal government to subsidize, to loan or provide stimulus money to any business, person, worker's union or any state; these issues must be regulated by the states. (Article I Section 8, Amendment X)**

"Whensoever the General Government assumes undelegated powers, its acts are unauthoritative, void, and of no force."

Thomas Jefferson

87. **The Constitution does not give our government the authority to dictate how a manufacturing company must build their product. We are a Republic, not a dictatorship.**
(Preamble, Article I Section 8, Article VI, Amendment X)

> *"Each State, in ratifying the Constitution, is considered as a sovereign body, independent of all others, and only to be bound by its own voluntary act. In this relation, then, the new Constitution will, if established, be a FEDERAL, and not a NATIONAL constitution."*

James Madison

88. **The government does not have the Constitutional authority to order any safe product off the market for the benefit of another so-called green product. (Article I Section 8)**

89. **We must abolish the power of the Human & Health Services Department that overburdens businesses for any reason, be it financial, health, or transportation issues.**

> *"Whensoever the General Government assumes undelegated powers, its acts are unauthoritative, void, and of no force."*

Thomas Jefferson

90. **College loans must be controlled by private businesses. Congress must dissolve all government**

owned companies and sell them to American owned companies or American private citizens.

"As wealth is power, so all power will infallibly draw wealth to itself by some means or other."

Edmund Burke

91. Medical insurance, welfare, housing and food stamp entitlements for the poor must be *slowly and wisely dissolved* and turned over to the states where they can work hand in hand with charities and churches to help the poor. These federal government departments are illegal!
(Article I Section 8, Amendment X)

92. The present Social Security, Medicare and Medicaid recipients must be taken care of within a new private system; the unconstitutional benevolent entities were created so that the politicians could control the people with promises and therefore get their votes to remain in office forever.
(Article I Section 8, Amendment X)

"I see,.... and with the deepest affliction, the rapid strides with which the federal branch of our government is advancing towards the usurpation of all the rights reserved to the States, and the consolidation in itself of all powers, foreign and domestic; and that, too, by constructions which, if legitimate, leave no limits to their power.... It is but too

evident that the three ruling branches of (the Federal government) are in combination to strip their colleagues, the State authorities, of the powers reserved by them, and to exercise themselves all functions foreign and domestic."

Thomas Jefferson

93. **We must abolish the minimum pay wage scale and any regulations that force businesses to pay medical insurance and other benefits to its employees.**
(Article I section 8 does not give Congress the power to dictate to a company nor the power to force any company to comply with any such unconstitutional mandates concerning business affairs.)

"The greatest danger to American freedom is a government that ignores the Constitution."

Thomas Jefferson

94. **It is time to abolish all federal laws and regulations on all the farmers and businesses of the country. Then we the people must stop the excessive, abusive state laws that also rule with the force of tyrants.**
(Article I Section 8)

This balance between the National and State governments ought to be dwelt on with peculiar attention, as it is of the utmost importance. It forms a double security to the people. If one encroaches on their rights they will find a powerful protection in the other. Indeed, they will both be prevented from overpassing their constitutional limits by a certain rivalship, which will ever subsist between them.

Alexander Hamilton

95. The Inheritance tax is immoral and this tyrannical death tax must be abolished forever.

Vocabulary

The intent for the vocabulary provided herein is that you will come to a clearer understanding of the words used in our Constitution, Declaration of Independence and the quotes of our Founding Fathers. Below is an example of an extended vocabulary usage in Article VI of the U.S Constitution.

Article VI
Actual Text of Second Paragraph

This Constitution, and the Laws of the United States which shall be made in Pursuance thereof; and all Treaties made, or which shall be made, under the Authority of the United States, shall be the supreme Law of the Land; and the Judges in every State shall be bound thereby, any Thing in the Constitution or Laws of any State to the Contrary notwithstanding.

Article VI
A Paraphrased Edition of Second Paragraph

This Constitution and all the laws of the United States that are in a continual process to accomplish the main design of the Constitution; and all the treaties made, or which shall be made under the Authority of two-thirds of the United States Senate and the President, everything in this Constitution shall be the supreme law of the land; and every judge in every state shall be bound to uphold the U. S. Constitution, that mandates a strictly limited federal government, along with all the indefinite number of urgently agreed to clauses in this Constitution that shall be applied to all the laws of any state, and no matter how contrary their laws, they must be changed to adhere to the principles that are written in the Constitution; every word shall be absolutely upheld, followed and obeyed.

Interpretation of Article VI by Robert Yates

"And by the sixth article, it is declared, "that this Constitution, and the laws of the United States, which shall be made in pursuance thereof, and the treaties made, or which shall be made, under the authority of the United States, shall be the supreme law of the land; and the judges in every State shall be bound thereby, any thing in the Constitution or law of any State to the contrary notwithstanding... there is no need of any intervention of the State governments, between the Congress and the people, to execute any one power vested in the general government, and that the Constitution

and laws of every State are nullified and declared void, so far as they are or shall be inconsistent with this Constitution, or the laws made in pursuance of it, or with treaties made under the authority of the United States. The government, then, so far as it extends, is a complete one, and not a confederation."

(Mr. Yates was a delegate to the Constitution Convention and a judge on the New York Supreme Court)

Vocabulary

Words used in the Declaration of Independence and Founding Fathers' quotes.

Chimerical: Imaginary; a fanciful, impossible idea.

Consanguinity: Family or descendants related by birth.

Definite Government: A **definite** government only issues laws that are easily understood and are **limited** only to what the **Constitution** allows. (Opposite is an **indefinite government** with Congress making any law they please and the President issuing executive orders.)

Despotism: A government with unlimited or unrestrained authority, an **arbitrary** government with the politicians unconcerned about **domestic tranquility** or their sworn oaths to uphold the **limited, definite** government that the **Constitution** mandates.

Evil: Evil is a profound, civil immorality and corrupt political traits which injure a nation, disturb the peace and impair the happiness and prosperity. **Evil** is when a politician uses lies and deception causing dissention in hopes to divide the nation's people to get his ideology made into law.

Moral: Capable of making the distinction between right and wrong in all areas of conduct, in decisions and in character that relates to religious teachings.

Tyranny: 1. Uses **arbitrary** or **despotic** (definition under the word Despotism), **oppressive** exercise of power over subjects with rigor not authorized or not requisite by the Constitution for the purposes of government.

2. **Oppressive** is synonymous with **tyranny.** It is a dominating government with overbearing taxes or services that weigh heavily on the people's spirits or senses with highly stressful, burdensome, overpowering pressure heaped upon *We the People.*

3. **Arbitrary** is when politicians do not govern by statute nor by the principles in the **Constitution**, but instead govern by their ideological preferences. All decisions are based upon a judge or court's notions, rather than in accordance with the **Constitution**.

Unconstitutional: illegal, disobeying the Supreme Law of the Land.

Usurp: To seize and hold in possession by force or without right.

Virtue: General moral goodness; right thinking and actions; uprightness, a quality that is regarded as good in philosophy and theology, excellence in general; merit; value. Pity is the virtue of law that tyrants use cruelly.

Yeomanry: Farmers who owned and cultivated their own land.

Constitution Vocabulary

Abridge, Abridging, Abridged: to diminish rights, depriving rights.
(Amendments I, XIV Section 1, XV Section 1, XIX, XXIV Section 1, and XXVI Section 1)

Any: an indefinite number.
(Article VI)

Appropriation: assigning to a particular use or special purpose.

Apportionment: dividing into just proportions.

Bill of Attainder: no legislation can convict a person or take away his possessions.
(Article I Section 9, 10)

Construed: to interpret in light of the proper meaning...**Amendment IX** says, neither the government, Congress, the President, nor the press shall make the words to mean differently than how the words were used in their arranged natural order. In other words, to understand the meaning of the words, you must arrange them as they were first written and interpret them as they were first defined.

(Article IV Section 3, Amendment IX)

Contrary Notwithstanding: Contrary—a law that is opposite of an agreed to proposition, such as the Constitution. **Notwithstanding**—refers to earlier sentences, clauses, which is everything written in the whole Constitution document that is the law of the land. Thus, no matter what you say or believe or what the law is in the states, all must conform to the Constitution.

(Article VI)

Disparage: To make inferior, to undervalue or treat with contempt, to injure. Per the words of **Amendment IX**, the government cannot deny or make inferior any of the people's rights, such as, all personal property or the tranquility in domestic life that is ordered to be free of government intervention as promised in the **Preamble.**

Domestic Tranquility: Domestic pertains to the nation considered as one family, their life's duties, affairs and concerns of life. **Tranquility** is that their life is free from agitation or disturbance caused by the government, as well as knowing that their government will not take away their standards of rights, property and just laws.

(Preamble)

Effects or Movables: Effects are goods; personal estate; **movables,** such as wares, commodities, furniture; any pieces of property not fixed, and thus not houses or land.

(Amendment IV)

Enumeration or Enumerated: an account of things that have been mentioned in previous amendments or articles.

(Amendment IX)

Ex Post Facto: after the fact—anything done before a law becomes a *known* law CANNOT be considered a crime.

(Article I Section 9, 10)

General Welfare: *We the People* have a constitutionally ordered exemption from unusual evil or calamity caused by government with the promised enjoyment and the peace of ordinary blessings of society and civil government, and free from government involvement in every aspect of our lives. In other words, the government's only role in our lives is to protect us from evil and calamity.

(Preamble, Article I Section 8)

Infringed: The government must not break, neglect, or violate by non-fulfillment. They must not hinder—not even a little bit.
(Amendment II)

Liberty: The freedom from government restraint. Civil liberties are those retained by laws that protect every person from injuring or controlling another. The opposite of liberty is tyranny that uses excessive laws and unnecessary regulations that hinder the public general welfare.
(Preamble, Amendment V & Amendment XIII Section I)

Marque and Reprisal: A commission that demands payment for injuries and empowers the state with the right to seize the land.
(Article I Section 10)

Militia: included all the people from the earliest age that one is capable to use firearms. All were to be well-armed with the latest weaponry that included those provided by the government so that every person would be able to protect the United States from foreign and domestic invaders. The fundamental law of the militia was created to support the constitution for all time. The militia organization and discipline rules were set by Congress, but Congress had no constitutional authority over the militia nor could they dissolve it or take away their weaponry.

The operation of the militia was under the authority of each state's government.
(Article I section 8, Amendment II)

Personal Rights: Man has a right to all his personal property. The government has no authority to seize or search without following Amendment IV. Each has the right to life, liberty and the pursuit of happiness without government intervention and each has the right to alter or abolish the government. It may be said that the people have a property in their rights.
(Amendment IV, IX)

Posterity: Descendants from one generation to all following generations.
(Preamble)

Property: Within people is a diversity of ability to invent, think, produce or buy something that then becomes an exclusive right; what they possess is legally their property. It is anything: papers, goods, money and profits from business, literary labors and ownership of lands, houses, cars, clothes, phones, computers, anything and everything.
(Amendment IV)

Pursuance: A process or a continual exertion to reach or accomplish the main design.
(Article VI)

Thing: A clause, a contract, an agreement or urgent statute agreed upon at a convention.
(Article IV)

Welfare: Refers to the lives of *We the People* living a life free from government intrusion. Allow the people to be a success and prosper without government help.
(Preamble)

INTRODUCTION
TO THE CONSTITUTION

Note the expert legal help written in the Blackstone Commentaries of 1803 by St. George Tucker that explains how we must apply the constitutionality questions concerning a particular power.

"Whenever, therefore, a question arises concerning the constitutionality of a particular power; the first question is, whether the power be expressed in the constitution? If it be, the question is decided. If it be not expressed, the next inquiry must be, whether it is properly an incident to an express power, and necessary to its execution. If it be, it may be exercised by congress. If it be not, congress cannot exercise it...And this construction of the words "necessary and proper," is not only consonant with that which prevailed during the discussions and ratification of the constitution, but is absolutely necessary to maintain their consistency with the peculiar character of the government, as possessed of particular and defined powers, only; not of the general and indefinite powers vested in ordinary governments.

Under this construction of the clause in question, it is calculated to operate as a powerful and immediate check upon the proceedings of the federal legislature, itself, so long as the sanction of an oath and the obligations of conscience, are regarded, among men."

St. George Tucker

Evidence of Government Tyranny

The President, Congress and the courts have specific, enumerated powers listed in the Constitution. These were the ONLY powers they had in order to benefit the general welfare of *We the people.* The meaning of general welfare in those days referred to allowing the people the freedom to make a living free from government intrusion in their lives. The government's only responsibility is to keep them safe from physical harm and to aid with roads, etc., for their prosperity. Read Article I Section 8 to find out there are only eighteen areas that Congress has power to control. Read Article II Section 2 & 3 to understand the President's limited powers. Read Article III Section 1-3 to find the areas of limited authority given to the Supreme Court. Any other area that these branches of government presently control beyond what is stated in the Constitution is unconstitutional, or in other words, ILLEGAL!

Note:

The underlined portions in parentheses in the following chapter are areas of the Constitution that have been amended. The number in parentheses that follow these portions are end notes found at the back of the chapter.

The U.S. Constitution

We the People of the United States, in Order to form a more perfect Union, establish Justice, insure domestic Tranquility, provide for the common defence, promote the general Welfare, and secure the Blessings of Liberty to ourselves and our Posterity, do ordain and establish this Constitution for the United States of America.

Article I

Section 1. All legislative Powers herein granted shall be vested in a Congress of the United States, which shall consist of a Senate and House of Representatives.

Section 2. The House of Representatives shall be composed of Members chosen every second Year by the People of the several States, and the Electors in each State shall have the Qualifications requisite for Electors of the most numerous Branch of the State Legislature.

No Person shall be a Representative who shall not have attained to the age of twenty five Years, and been seven

Years a Citizen of the United States, and who shall not, when elected, be an Inhabitant of that State in which he shall be chosen.

(Representatives and direct Taxes shall be apportioned among the several States which may be included within this Union, according to their respective Numbers, which shall be determined by adding to the whole Number of free Persons, including those bound to Service for a Term of Years, and excluding Indians not taxed, three fifths of all other Persons.) (1) The actual Enumeration shall be made within three Years after the first Meeting of the Congress of the United States, and within every subsequent Term of ten Years, in such Manner as they shall by Law direct. The Number of Representatives shall not exceed one for every thirty Thousand, but each State shall have at Least one Representative; and until such enumeration shall be made, the State of New Hampshire shall be entitled to chuse three, Massachusetts eight, Rhode-Island and Providence Plantations one, Connecticut five, New-York six, New Jersey four, Pennsylvania eight, Delaware one, Maryland six, Virginia ten, North Carolina five, South Carolina five, and Georgia three.

When vacancies happen in the Representation from any State, the Executive Authority thereof shall issue Writs of Election to fill such Vacancies.

The House of Representatives shall chuse their Speaker and other Officers; and shall have the sole Power of Impeachment.

Section 3. The Senate of the United States shall be composed of two Senators from each State, <u>(chosen by the Legislature thereof,) (2)</u> for six Years; and each Senator shall have one Vote.

Immediately after they shall be assembled in Consequence of the first Election, they shall be divided as equally as may be into three Classes. The Seats of the Senators of the first Class shall be vacated at the Expiration of the second Year, of the second Class at the Expiration of the fourth Year, and the third Class at the Expiration of the sixth Year, so that one third may be chosen every second Year; <u>(and if Vacancies happen by Resignation, or otherwise, during the Recess of the Legislature of any State, the Executive thereof may make temporary Appointments until the next Meeting of the Legislature, which shall then fill such Vacancies.) (3)</u>

No Person shall be a Senator who shall not have attained to the Age of thirty Years, and been nine Years a Citizen of the United States and who shall not, when elected, be an Inhabitant of that State for which he shall be chosen.

The Vice President of the United States shall be President of the Senate, but shall have no Vote, unless they be equally divided.

The Senate shall chuse their other Officers, and also a President pro tempore, in the Absence of the Vice President, or when he shall exercise the Office of President of the United States.

The Senate shall have the sole Power to try all Impeachments. When sitting for that Purpose, they shall be on Oath or Affirmation. When the President of the United States is tried, the Chief Justice shall preside: And no Person shall be convicted without the Concurrence of two thirds of the Members present.

Judgment in Cases of Impeachment shall not extend further than to removal from Office, and disqualification to hold and enjoy any Office of Honor, Trust or Profit under the United States: but the Party convicted shall nevertheless be liable and subject to Indictment, Trial, Judgment and Punishment, according to Law.

Section 4. The Times, Places and Manner of hold-ing Elections for Senators and Representatives, shall be prescribed in each State by the Legislature thereof; but the Congress may at any time by Law make or alter such Regulations, except as to the Places of chusing Senators.

The Congress shall assemble at least once in every Year, and such Meeting shall be (on the first Monday in December,) (4) unless they shall by Law appoint a different Day.

Section 5. Each House shall be the Judge of the Elections, Returns and Qualifications of its own Members, and a Majority of each shall constitute a Quorum to do Business; but a smaller Number may adjourn from day to day, and may be authorized to compel the Attendance of absent Members, in such Manner, and under such Penalties as each House may provide.

Each House may determine the Rules of its Proceedings, punish its Members for disorderly Behaviour, and, with the Concurrence of two thirds, expel a Member.

Each House shall keep a Journal of its Proceedings, and from time to time publish the same, excepting such Parts as may in their Judgment require Secrecy; and the Yeas and Nays of the Members of either House on any question shall, at the Desire of one fifth of those Present, be entered on the Journal.

Neither House, during the Session of Congress, shall, without the Consent of the other, adjourn for more than three days, nor to any other Place than that in which the two Houses shall be sitting.

Section 6. The Senators and Representatives shall receive a Compensation for their Services, to be ascertained by Law, and paid out of the Treasury of the United States. They shall in all Cases, except Treason, Felony and Breach of the Peace, be privileged from Arrest during their Attendance at the Session of their respective Houses, and in going to and returning from the same; and for any Speech or Debate in either House, they shall not be questioned in any other Place.

No Senator or Representative shall, during the Time for which he was elected, be appointed to any civil Office under the Authority of the United States, which shall have been created, or the Emoluments whereof shall have been encreased during such time: and no Person holding any Office under the United States, shall be a Member of either House during his Continuance in Office.

Section 7. All Bills for raising Revenue shall originate in the House of Representatives; but the Senate may propose or concur with Amendments as on other Bills.

Every Bill which shall have passed the House of Representatives and the Senate, shall, before it become a Law, be presented to the President of the United States; if he approve he shall sign it, but if not he shall return it, with his Objections to that House in which it shall have originated, who shall enter the Objections at large on their Journal, and proceed to reconsider it. If after such Reconsideration two thirds of that House shall agree to pass the Bill, it shall be sent, together with the Objections, to the other House, by which it shall likewise be reconsidered, and if approved by two thirds of that House, it shall become a Law. But in all such Cases the Votes of both Houses shall be determined by Yeas and Nays, and the Names of the Persons voting for and against the Bill shall be entered on the Journal of each House respectively. If any Bill shall not be returned by the President within ten Days (Sundays excepted) after it shall have been presented to him, the Same shall be a Law, in like Manner as if he had signed it, unless the Congress by their Adjournment prevent its Return, in which Case it shall not be a Law.

Every Order, Resolution, or Vote to which the Concurrence of the Senate and House of Representatives may be necessary (except on a question of Adjournment) shall be presented to the President of the United States; and before the Same shall take Effect, shall be approved by him, or being disapproved by him, shall be repassed by two thirds of the Senate and House of Representatives, according to the Rules and Limitations prescribed in the Case of a Bill.

Section 8. The Congress shall have Power To lay and collect Taxes, Duties, Imposts and Excises, to pay the Debts and provide for the common Defence and general Welfare of the United States; but all Duties, Imposts and Excises shall be uniform throughout the United States;

To borrow Money on the credit of the United States;

To regulate Commerce with foreign Nations, and among the several States, and with the Indian Tribes;

To establish an uniform Rule of Naturalization, and uniform Laws on the subject of Bankruptcies throughout the United States;

To coin Money, regulate the Value thereof, and of foreign Coin, and fix the Standard of Weights and Measures;

To provide for the Punishment of counterfeiting the Securities and current Coin of the United States;

To establish Post Offices and post Roads;

To promote the Progress of Science and useful Arts, by securing for limited Times to Authors and Inventors the exclusive Right to their respective Writings and Discoveries;

To constitute Tribunals inferior to the supreme Court;

To define and punish Piracies and Felonies committed on the high Seas, and Offences against the Law of Nations;

To declare War, grant Letters of Marque and Reprisal, and make Rules concerning Captures on Land and Water;

To raise and support Armies, but no Appropriation of Money to that Use shall be for a longer Term than two Years;

To provide and maintain a Navy;

To make Rules for the Government and Regulation of the land and naval Forces;

To provide for calling forth the Militia to execute the Laws of the Union, suppress Insurrections and repel Invasions;

To provide for organizing, arming, and disciplining, the Militia, and for governing such Part of them as may be employed in the Service of the United States, reserving to the States respectively, the Appointment of the Officers, and the Authority of training the Militia according to the discipline prescribed by Congress;

To exercise exclusive Legislation in all Cases whatsoever, over such District (not exceeding ten Miles square) as may, by Cession of particular States, and the Acceptance of Congress, become the Seat of the Government of the United States, and to exercise like Authority over all Places purchased by the Consent of the Legislature of the State in which the Same shall be, for the Erection of Forts, Magazines, Arsenals, dock-Yards, and other needful Buildings;–And

To make all Laws which shall be necessary and proper for carrying into Execution the foregoing Powers, and all other Powers vested by this Constitution in the Government of the United States, or in any Department or Officer thereof.

Section 9. The Migration or Importation of such Persons as any of the States now existing shall think proper to admit, shall not be prohibited by the Congress prior to the Year one thousand eight hundred and eight, but a Tax or duty may be imposed on such Importation, not exceeding ten dollars for each Person.

The Privilege of the Writ of Habeas Corpus shall not be suspended, unless when in Cases of Rebellion or Invasion the public Safety may require it.

No Bill of Attainder or ex post facto Law shall be passed.

No Capitation, or other direct, Tax shall be laid, <u>(unless in Proportion to the Census or Enumeration herein before directed to be taken.) (5)</u>

No Tax or Duty shall be laid on Articles exported from any State.

No Preference shall be given by any Regulation of Commerce or Revenue to the Ports of one State over those of another: nor shall Vessels bound to, or from, one State, be obliged to enter, clear or pay Duties in another.

No Money shall be drawn from the Treasury, but in Consequence of Appropriations made by Law; and a regular Statement and Account of Receipts and Expenditures of all public Money shall be published from time to time.

No Title of Nobility shall be granted by the United States: And no Person holding any Office of Profit or Trust under them, shall, without the Consent of the Congress, accept of any present, Emolument, Office, or Title, of any kind whatever, from any King, Prince, or foreign State.

Section 10. No State shall enter into any Treaty, Alliance, or Confederation; grant Letters of Marque and

Reprisal; coin Money; emit Bills of Credit; make any Thing but gold and silver Coin a Tender in Payment of Debts; pass any Bill of Attainder, ex post facto Law, or Law impairing the Obligation of Contracts, or grant any Title of Nobility.

No State shall, without the Consent of the Congress, lay any Imposts or Duties on Imports or Exports, except what may be absolutely necessary for executing it's inspection Laws: and the net Produce of all Duties and Imposts, laid by any State on Imports or Exports, shall be for the Use of the Treasury of the United States; and all such Laws shall be subject to the Revision and Controul of the Congress.

No State shall, without the Consent of Congress, lay any Duty of Tonnage, keep Troops, or Ships of War in time of Peace, enter into any Agreement or Compact with another State, or with a foreign Power, or engage in War, unless actually invaded, or in such imminent Danger as will not admit of delay.

Article II

Section 1. The executive Power shall be vested in a President of the United States of America. He shall hold his Office during the Term of four Years, and, together with the Vice President, chosen for the same Term, be elected, as follows:

Each State shall appoint, in such Manner as the Legislature thereof may direct, a Number of Electors, equal to the whole Number of Senators and Representatives to

which the State may be entitled in the Congress: but no
Senator or Representative, or Person holding an Office of
Trust or Profit under the United States, shall be appointed
an Elector.

(The Electors shall meet in their respective States, and
vote by Ballot for two Persons, of whom one at least shall
not be an Inhabitant of the same State with themselves. And
they shall make a List of all the Persons voted for, and of the
Number of Votes for each; which List they shall sign and
certify, and transmit sealed to the Seat of the Government of
the United States, directed to the President of the Senate. The
President of the Senate shall, in the Presence of the Senate and
House of Representatives, open all the Certificates, and the
Votes shall then be counted. The Person having the greatest
Number of Votes shall be the President, if such Number be a
Majority of the whole Number of Electors appointed; and if
there be more than one who have such Majority, and have an
equal Number of Votes, then the House of Representatives
shall immediately chuse by Ballot one of them for President;
and if no Person have a Majority, then from the five highest on the List the said House shall in like Manner chuse
the President. But in chusing the President, the Votes shall
be taken by States, the Representation from each State having one Vote; A quorum for this Purpose shall consist of a
Member or Members from two thirds of the States, and a
Majority of all the States shall be necessary to a Choice. In
every Case, after the Choice of the President, the Person having the greatest Number of Votes of the Electors shall be the

<u>Vice President. But if there should remain two or more who have equal Votes, the Senate shall chuse from them by Ballot the Vice President.) (6)</u>

The Congress may determine the Time of chusing the Electors, and the Day on which they shall give their Votes; which Day shall be the same throughout the United States.

No Person except a natural born Citizen, or a Citizen of the United States, at the time of the Adoption of this Constitution, shall be eligible to the Office of President; neither shall any Person be eligible to that Office who shall not have attained to the Age of thirty five Years, and been fourteen Years a Resident within the United States.

<u>(In Case of the Removal of the President from Office, or of his Death, Resignation, or Inability to discharge the Powers and Duties of the said Office, the Same shall devolve on the Vice President, and the Congress may by Law provide for the Case of Removal, Death, Resignation or Inability, both of the President and Vice President, declaring what Officer shall then act as President, and such Officer shall act accordingly, until the Disability be removed, or a President shall be elected.) (7)</u>

The President shall, at stated Times, receive for his Services, a Compensation, which shall neither be encreased nor diminished during the Period for which he shall have been elected, and he shall not receive within that Period any other Emolument from the United States, or any of them.

Before he enter on the Execution of his Office, he shall take the following Oath or Affirmation:–"I do solemnly swear (or affirm) that I will faithfully execute the Office of President of the United States, and will to the best of my Ability, preserve, protect and defend the Constitution of the United States."

Section 2. The President shall be Commander in Chief of the Army and Navy of the United States, and of the Militia of the several States, when called into the actual Service of the United States; he may require the Opinion, in writing, of the principal Officer in each of the executive Departments, upon any Subject relating to the Duties of their respective Offices, and he shall have Power to grant Reprieves and Pardons for Offences against the United States, except in Cases of Impeachment.

He shall have Power, by and with the Advice and Consent of the Senate, to make Treaties, provided two thirds of the Senators present concur; and he shall nominate, and by and with the Advice and Consent of the Senate, shall appoint Ambassadors, other public Ministers and Consuls, Judges of the supreme Court, and all other Officers of the United States, whose Appointments are not herein otherwise pro-vided for, and which shall be established by Law: but the Congress may by Law vest the Appointment of such inferior Officers, as they think proper, in the President alone, in the Courts of Law, or in the Heads of Departments.

The President shall have Power to fill up all Vacancies that may happen during the Recess of the Senate, by granting

Commissions which shall expire at the End of their next Session.

Section 3. He shall from time to time give to the Congress Information of the State of the Union, and recommend to their Consideration such Measures as he shall judge necessary and expedient; he may, on extraordinary Occasions, convene both Houses, or either of them, and in Case of Disagreement between them, with Respect to the Time of Adjournment, he may adjourn them to such Time as he shall think proper; he shall receive Ambassadors and other public Ministers; he shall take Care that the Laws be faithfully executed, and shall Commission all the Officers of the United States.

Section 4. The President, Vice President and all civil Officers of the United States, shall be removed from Office on Impeachment for, and Conviction of, Treason, Bribery, or other high Crimes and Misdemeanors.

Article III

Section 1. The judicial Power of the United States, shall be vested in one supreme Court, and in such inferior Courts as the Congress may from time to time ordain and establish. The Judges, both of the supreme and inferior Courts, shall hold their Offices during good Behaviour, and shall, at stated Times, receive for their Services, a Compensation, which shall not be diminished during their Continuance in Office.

Section 2. The judicial Power shall extend to all Cases, in Law and Equity, arising under this Constitution, the Laws of the United States, and Treaties made, or which shall be made, under their Authority;–to all Cases affecting Ambassadors, other public Ministers and Consuls;–to all Cases of admiralty and maritime Jurisdiction;–to Controversies to which the United States shall be a Party;–to Controversies between two or more States;–(between a State and Citizens of another State;) (8)–between Citizens of different States;–between Citizens of the same State claiming Lands under Grants of different States, (and between a State, or the Citizens thereof, and foreign States, Citizens or Subjects.) (8)

In all Cases affecting Ambassadors, other public Ministers and Consuls, and those in which a State shall be Party, the supreme Court shall have original Jurisdiction. In all the other Cases before mentioned, the supreme Court shall have appellate Jurisdiction, both as to Law and Fact, with such Exceptions, and under such Regulations as the Congress shall make.

The Trial of all Crimes, except in Cases of Impeachment, shall be by Jury; and such Trial shall be held in the State where the said Crimes shall have been committed; but when not committed within any State, the Trial shall be at such Place or Places as the Congress may by Law have directed.

Section 3. Treason against the United States, shall consist only in levying War against them, or in adhering to their Enemies, giving them Aid and Comfort. No Person shall be convicted of Treason unless on the Testimony of two Witnesses to the same overt Act, or on Confession in open Court.

The Congress shall have Power to declare the Punishment of Treason, but no Attainder of Treason shall work Corruption of Blood, or Forfeiture except during the Life of the Person attainted.

Article IV

Section 1. Full Faith and Credit shall be given in each State to the public Acts, Records, and judicial Proceedings of every other State. And the Congress may by general Laws prescribe the Manner in which such Acts, Records, and Proceedings shall be proved, and the Effect thereof.

Section 2. The Citizens of each State shall be entitled to all Privileges and Immunities of Citizens in the several States.

A Person charged in any State with Treason, Felony, or other Crime, who shall flee from Justice, and be found in another State, shall on Demand of the executive Authority of the State from which he fled, be delivered up, to be removed to the State having Jurisdiction of the Crime.

(No Person held to Service or Labour in one State, under the Laws thereof, escaping into another, shall, in Consequence of any Law or Regulation therein, be discharged from such Service or Labour, but shall be delivered up on Claim of the Party to whom such Service or Labour may be due.) (9)

Section 3. New States may be admitted by the Congress into this Union; but no new States shall be formed or erected within the Jurisdiction of any other State; nor any State be formed by the Junction of two or more States, or Parts of States, without the Consent of the Legislatures of the States concerned as well as of the Congress.

The Congress shall have Power to dispose of and make all needful Rules and Regulations respecting the Territory or other Property belonging to the United States; and nothing in this Constitution shall be so construed as to Prejudice any Claims of the United States, or of any particular State.

Section 4. The United States shall guarantee to every State in this Union a Republican Form of Government, and shall protect each of them against Invasion; and on Application of the Legislature, or of the Executive (when the Legislature cannot be convened) against domestic Violence.

Article V

The Congress, whenever two thirds of both Houses shall deem it necessary, shall propose Amendments to this Constitution, or, on the Application of the Legislatures of two thirds of the several States, shall call a Convention for proposing Amendments, which, in either Case, shall be valid to all Intents and Purposes, as Part of this Constitution, when ratified by the Legislatures of three fourths of the several States, or by Conventions in three fourths thereof, as the one or the other Mode of Ratification may be proposed by the Congress; Provided that no Amendment which may be made prior to the Year One thousand eight hundred and eight shall in any Manner affect the first and fourth Clauses in the Ninth Section of the first Article; and that no State, without its Consent, shall be deprived of its equal Suffrage in the Senate.

Article VI

All Debts contracted and Engagements entered into, before the Adoption of this Constitution, shall be as valid against the United States under this Constitution, as under the Confederation.

This Constitution, and the Laws of the United States which shall be made in Pursuance thereof; and all Treaties made, or which shall be made, under the Authority of the United States, shall be the supreme Law of the Land; and the Judges in every State shall be bound thereby, any Thing in the Constitution or Laws of any State to the Contrary notwithstanding.

The Senators and Representatives before mentioned, and the Members of the several State Legislatures, and all executive and judicial Officers, both of the United States and of the several States, shall be bound by Oath or Affirmation, to support this Constitution; but no religious Test shall ever be required as a Qualification to any Office or public Trust under the United States.

Article VII

The Ratification of the Conventions of nine States, shall be sufficient for the Establishment of this Constitution between the States so ratifying the Same.

Done in Convention by the Unanimous Consent of the States present the Seventeenth Day of September in the Year of our Lord one thousand seven hundred and Eighty seven and of the Independence of the United States of America the Twelfth In witness whereof We have hereunto subscribed our Names,

Go. Washington–Presidt. and deputy from Virginia
New Hampshire: John Langdon, Nicholas Gilman
Massachusetts: Nathaniel Gorham, Rufus King

Connecticut: William Samuel Johnson, Roger Sherman

New York: Alexander Hamilton

New Jersey: William Livingston, David Brearly, William Paterson, Jonathan Dayton

Pennsylvania: Benjamin Franklin, Thomas Mifflin, Robert Morris, George Clymer, Thomas FitzSimons, Jared Ingersoll, James Wilson, Gouverneur Morris

Delaware: George Read, Gunning Bedford, Jr., John Dickinson, Richard Bassett, Jacob Broom

Maryland: James McHenry, Daniel of Saint Thomas Jenifer, Daniel Carroll

Virginia: John Blair, James Madison, Jr.

North Carolina: William Blount, Richard Dobbs Spaight, Hugh Williamson

South Carolina: John Rutledge, Charles Cotesworth Pinckney, Charles Pinckney, Pierce Butler

Georgia: William Few, Abraham Baldwin

(1) Changed by section 2 of Amendment XIV.

(2) Changed by Amendment XVII.

(3) Changed by Amendment XVII.

(4) Changed by section 2 of Amendment XX.

(5) See Amendment XVI.

(6) Changed by Amendment XII.

(7) Changed by Amendment XXV.

(8) Changed by Amendment XI.

(9) Changed by Amendment XIII.

The Amendments to the Constitution of the United States of America

Amendment I

Congress shall make no law respecting an establishment of religion, or prohibiting the free exercise thereof; or abridging the freedom of speech, or of the press; or the right of the people peaceably to assemble, and to petition the Government for a redress of grievances.

Amendment II

A well regulated militia, being necessary to the security of a free State, the right of the people to keep and bear arms, shall not be infringed.

Amendment III

No soldier shall, in time of peace be quartered in any house, without the consent of the owner, nor in time of war, but in a manner to be prescribed by law.

Amendment IV

The right of the people to be secure in their persons, houses, papers, and effects, against unreasonable searches and seizures, shall not be violated, and no warrants shall issue, but upon probable cause, supported by oath or affirmation, and particularly describing the place to be searched, and the persons or things to be seized.

Amendment V

No person shall be held to answer for a capital, or otherwise infamous crime, unless on a presentment or indictment of a Grand Jury, except in cases arising in the land or naval forces, or in the militia, when in actual service in time of war or public danger; nor shall any person be subject for the same offence to be twice put in jeopardy of life or limb; nor shall be compelled in any criminal case to be a witness, against himself, nor be deprived of life, liberty, or property, without due process of law; nor shall private property be taken for public use, without just compensation.

Amendment VI

In all criminal prosecutions, the accused shall enjoy the right to a speedy and public trial, by an impartial jury of the State and district wherein the crime shall have been committed, which district shall have been previously ascertained by law, and to be informed of the nature and cause of the accusation; to be confronted with the witnesses against him; to have compulsory process for obtaining witnesses in his favor, and to have the assistance of counsel for his defense.

Amendment VII

In suits at common law, where the value in controversy shall exceed twenty dollars, the right of trial by jury shall be preserved, and no fact tried by a jury, shall be otherwise re-examined in any court of the United States, than according to the rules of the common law.

Amendment VIII

Excessive bail shall not be required, nor excessive fines imposed, nor cruel and unusual punishments inflicted.

Amendment IX

The enumeration in the Constitution, of certain rights, shall not be construed to deny or disparage others retained by the people.

Amendment X

The powers not delegated to the United States by the Constitution, nor prohibited by it to the States, are reserved to the States, respectively, or to the people.

Amendments I through X (known as the Bill of Rights) were ratified effective December 15, 1791

Amendment XI

Ratified Feb. 7, 1795

The judicial power of the United States shall not be construed to extend to any suit in law or equity, commenced or prosecuted against one of the United States by citizens of another State, or by citizens or subjects of any foreign state.

Amendment XII

Ratified July 27, 1804

The electors shall meet in their respective states, and vote by ballot for President and Vice President, one of whom, at least, shall not be an inhabitant of the same state with themselves; they shall name in their ballots the person voted for as President, and in distinct ballots the person voted for as Vice President, and they shall make distinct lists of all persons voted for as President, and of all persons voted for as Vice President, and of the number of votes for each, which lists they shall sign and certify, and transmit sealed to the seat of the government of the United States, directed to the President of the Senate; the President of the Senate shall, in the presence of the Senate and House of Representatives, open all the certificates and the votes shall then be counted; the person having the greatest number of votes for President, shall be the President, if such number be a majority of the whole number of electors appointed; and if no person have such majority, then from the persons having the highest numbers not exceeding three on the list of those voted for as President, the House of Representatives shall choose immediately, by ballot, the President. But in choosing the President, the votes shall be taken by states, the representation from each State having one vote; a quorum for this purpose shall consist of a member or members from two thirds of the states, and a majority of all the states shall be necessary to a choice. (And if the House of Representatives shall not choose a President whenever the right of choice shall devolve upon them, before the fourth day of March next following, then the Vice President shall act as President, as in the case of the death or other constitutional disability of the President.) (10) The person having the greatest number of votes as Vice President, shall be the Vice President, if such number be a majority of the whole number of electors appointed, and if no person have a majority, then from the two highest numbers on the list, the Senate shall choose the Vice President; a quorum for the purpose shall consist of two thirds of the whole number of Senators, and a majority of the whole number shall be necessary to a choice. But no person constitutionally ineligible to the office of President shall be eligible to that of Vice President of the United States.

Amendment XIII
Ratified Dec. 6, 1865

Section 1. Neither slavery nor involuntary servitude, except as a punishment for crime whereof the party shall have been duly convicted, shall exist within the United States, or any place subject to their jurisdiction.

Section 2. Congress shall have power to enforce this article by appropriate legislation.

Amendment XIV
Ratified July 9, 1868

Section 1. All persons born or naturalized in the United States, and subject to the jurisdiction thereof, are citizens of the United States and of the State wherein they reside. No State shall make or enforce any law which shall abridge the privileges or immunities of citizens of the United States; nor shall any State deprive any person of life, liberty, or property, without due process of law; nor deny to any person within its jurisdiction the equal protection of the laws.

Section 2. Representatives shall be apportioned among the several States according to their respective numbers, counting the whole number of persons in each State, excluding Indians not taxed. But when the right to vote at any election for the choice of electors for President and Vice President of the United States, Representatives in Congress, the executive and judicial officers of a State, or the members of the Legislature thereof, is denied to any of the male inhabitants of such State, being twenty-one years of age, and citizens of the United States, or in any way abridged, except for participation in rebellion, or other crime, the basis of representation therein shall be reduced in the proportion which the number of such male citizens shall bear to the whole number of male citizens twenty-one years of age in such State.

Section 3. No person shall be a Senator or Representative in Congress, or elector of President and Vice President, or hold any office, civil or military, under the United States, or under any State, who, having previously taken an oath, as a member of Congress, or as an officer of the United States, or as a member of any State Legislature, or as an executive or judicial officer of any State, to support the Constitution of the United States, shall have engaged in insurrection or rebellion against the same, or given aid or comfort to the enemies thereof. But Congress may, by a vote of two thirds of each House, remove such disability.

Section 4. The validity of the public debt of the United States, authorized by law, including debts incurred for payment of pensions and bounties for services in suppressing insurrection or rebellion, shall not be questioned. But neither the United States nor any State shall assume or pay any debt or obligation incurred in aid of insurrection or rebellion against the United States, or any claim for the loss or emancipation of any slave; but all such debts, obligations, and claims shall be held illegal and void.

Section 5. The Congress shall have power to enforce, by appropriate legislation, the provisions of this article.

Amendment XV
Ratified Feb. 3, 1870

Section 1. The right of citizens of the United States to vote shall not be denied or abridged by the United States or by any State on account of race, color, or previous condition of servitude.

Section 2. The Congress shall have power to enforce this article by appropriate legislation.

Amendment XVI
Ratified Feb. 3, 1913

The Congress shall have power to lay and collect taxes on incomes, from whatever source derived, without apportionment among the several States, and without regard to any census or enumeration.

Amendment XVII
Ratified April 8, 1913

The Senate of the United States shall be composed of two Senators from each State, elected by the people thereof, for six years; and each Senator shall have one vote. The electors in each State shall have the qualifications requisite for electors of the most numerous branch of the State Legislatures.

When vacancies happen in the representation of any State in the Senate, the executive authority of such State shall issue writs of election to fill such vacancies: Provided, that the legislature of any State may empower the executive thereof to make temporary appointment until the people fill the vacancies by election as the legislature may direct.

This amendment shall not be so construed as to affect the election or term of any Senator chosen before it becomes valid as part of the Constitution.

Amendment XVIII
Ratified Jan. 16, 1919

(Section 1. After one year from the ratification of this article the manufacture, sale, or transportation of intoxicating liquors within, the importation thereof into, or the exportation thereof from the United States and all territory subject to the jurisdiction thereof for beverage purposes is hereby prohibited.

Section 2. The Congress and the several States shall have concurrent power to enforce this article by appropriate legislation.

Section 3. This article shall be inoperative unless it shall have been ratified as an amendment to the Constitution by the legislatures of the several States, as provided in the Constitution, within seven years from the date of the submission hereof to the States by Congress.) (11)

Amendment XIX
Ratified Aug. 18, 1920

The right of citizens of the United States to vote shall not be denied or abridged by the United States or by any State on account of sex.

Congress shall have power to enforce this article by appropriate legislation.

Amendment XX
Ratified Jan. 23, 1933

Section 1. The terms of the President and Vice President shall end at noon on the twentieth day of January, and the terms of Senators and Representatives at noon on the third day of January, of the years in which such terms would have ended if this article had not been ratified; and the terms of their successors shall then begin.

Section 2. The Congress shall assemble at least once in every year, and such meeting shall begin at noon on the third day of January, unless they shall by law appoint a different day.

Section 3. If, at the time fixed for the beginning of the term of the President, the President-elect shall have died, the Vice President-elect shall become President. If a President shall not have been chosen before the time fixed for the beginning of his term, or if the President-elect shall have failed to qualify, then the Vice President shall have qualified; and the Congress may by law provide for the case wherein neither a President-elect nor a Vice President-elect shall have qualified, declaring who shall then act as President, or the manner in which one who is to act shall be selected, and such person shall act accordingly until a President or Vice President shall have qualified.

Section 4. The Congress may by law provide for the case of the death of any of the persons from whom the House of Representatives may choose a President whenever the right of choice shall have devolved upon them, and for the case of the death of any of the persons from whom the Senate may choose a Vice President whenever the right of choice shall have devolved upon them.

Section 5. Sections 1 and 2 shall take effect on the 15th day of October following the ratification of this article.

Section 6. This article shall be inoperative unless it shall have been ratified as an amendment to the Constitution by the legislatures of three fourths of the several States within seven years from the date of its submission.

Amendment XXI
Ratified Dec. 5, 1933

Section 1. The eighteenth article of amendment to the Constitution of the United States is hereby repealed.

Section 2. The transportation or importation into any State, territory, or possession of the United States for delivery or use therein of intoxicating liquors, in violation of the laws thereof, is hereby prohibited.

Section 3. This article shall be inoperative unless it shall have been ratified as an amendment to the Constitution by convention in the several States, as provided in the Constitution, within seven years from the date of the submission thereof to the States by the Congress.

Amendment XXII
Ratified Feb. 27, 1951

Section 1. No person shall be elected to the office of the President more than twice, and no person who has held the office of President, or acted as President, for more than two years of a term to which some other person was elected President shall be elected to the office of the President more than once. But this article shall not apply to any person holding the office of President when this article was proposed by the Congress, and shall not prevent any person who may be holding the office of President, or acting as President, during the term within which this article becomes operative from holding the office of President or acting as President during the remainder of such term.

Section 2. This article shall be inoperative unless it shall have been ratified as an amendment to the Constitution by the legislatures of three fourths of the several States within seven years from the date of its submission to the States by the Congress.

Amendment XXIII
Ratified March 29, 1961

Section 1. The District constituting the seat of Government of the United States shall appoint in such manner as the Congress may direct: A number of electors of President and Vice President equal to the whole number of Senators and Representatives in Congress to which the District would be entitled if it were a State, but in no event more than the least populous State; they shall be in addition to those appointed by the States, but they shall be considered, for the purposes of the election of President and Vice President, to be electors appointed by a State; and they shall meet in the District and perform such duties as provided by the twelfth article of amendment.

Section 2. The Congress shall have the power to enforce this article by appropriate legislation.

Amendment XXIV
Ratified Jan. 23, 1964

Section 1. The right of citizens of the United States to vote in any primary or other election for President or Vice President, for electors for President or Vice President, or for

Senator or Representative in Congress, shall not be denied or abridged by the United States or any State by reasons of failure to pay any poll tax or other tax.

Section 2. The Congress shall have the power to enforce this article by appropriate legislation.

Amendment XXV
Ratified Feb. 10, 1967

Section 1. In case of the removal of the President from office or of his death or resignation, the Vice President shall become President.

Section 2. Whenever there is a vacancy in the office of the Vice President, the President shall nominate a Vice President who shall take office upon confirmation by a majority vote of both Houses of Congress.

Section 3. Whenever the President transmits to the President pro tempore of the Senate and the Speaker of the House of Representatives his written declaration that he is unable to discharge the powers and duties of his office, and until he transmits to them a written declaration to the contrary, such powers and duties shall be discharged by the Vice President as Acting President.

Section 4. Whenever the Vice President and a majority of either the principal officers of the executive departments or of such other body as Congress may by law provide, transmit to the President pro tempore of the Senate and the Speaker of the House of Representatives their written declaration that the President is unable to discharge the powers and duties of his office, the Vice President shall immediately assume the powers and duties of the office as Acting President.

Thereafter, when the President transmits to the President pro tempore of the Senate and the Speaker of the House of Representatives his written declaration that no inability exists, he shall resume the powers and duties of his office unless the Vice President and a majority of either the principal officers of the executive department or of such other body as Congress may by law provide, transmit within four days to the President pro tempore of the Senate and the Speaker of the House of Representatives their written declaration that the President is unable to discharge the powers and duties of his office. Thereupon Congress shall decide the issue, assembling within forty-eight hours for that purpose if not in session. If the Congress, within twenty-one days after receipt of the latter written declaration, or, if Congress is not in session, within twenty-one days after Congress is required to assemble, determines by two thirds vote of both Houses that the President is unable to discharge the powers and duties of his office, the Vice President shall continue to discharge the same as Acting President; otherwise, the President shall resume the powers and duties of his office.

Amendment XXVI
Ratified July 1, 1971

Section 1. The right of citizens of the United States, who are 18 years of age or older, to vote shall not be denied or abridged by the United States or by any state on account of age.

Section 2. The Congress shall have power to enforce this article by appropriate legislation.

Amendment XXVII
Ratified May 7, 1992

No law, varying the compensation for the services of the Senators and Representatives, shall take effect, until an election of Representatives shall have intervened.

(10) Superseded by section 3 of Amendment XX.

(11) The Eighteenth Amendment repealed by Amendment XXI.

THE DECLARATION OF INDEPENDENCE

Note: in the original Declaration of Independence, our Founding Fathers listed 29 abuses done by the King of Great Britain which finally encouraged them to declare American independence. Although the Founders did not originally number the grievances, I have numbered 19 that align with 19 of my own similar grievances against our present day government. Following the Declaration of Independence, those 19 similar grievances are listed and elaborated.

Declaration of Independence
The unanimous Declaration of the thirteen united States of America, in Congress, July 4, 1776.

When in the Course of human events, it becomes necessary for one people to dissolve the political bands which have connected them with another, and to assume among the powers of the earth, the separate and equal station to which the Laws of Nature and of Nature's God entitle them, a decent respect to the opinions of mankind requires that they should declare the causes which impel them to the separation.

We hold these truths to be self-evident, that all men are created equal, that they are endowed by their Creator with certain unalienable Rights, that among these are Life, Liberty and the pursuit of Happiness—That to secure these rights, Governments are instituted among Men, deriving their just powers from the consent of the governed, that whenever any Form of Government becomes destructive of these ends, it is the Right of the People to alter or to abolish it, and to institute new Government, laying its foundation on such principles and organizing its powers in such form, as to them shall seem most likely to effect their Safety and Happiness. Prudence, indeed, will dictate that Governments long established should not be changed for light and transient causes; and accordingly all experience hath shewn, that mankind are more disposed to suffer, while evils are sufferable, than to right themselves by abolishing the forms to which they are accustomed. But when a long train of abuses and usurpations, pursuing invariably the same Object evinces a design to reduce them under absolute Despotism, it is their right, it is their duty, to throw off such Government, and to provide new Guards for their future security.—Such has been the patient sufferance of these Colonies; and such is now the necessity which constrains them to alter their former Systems of Government. The history of the present King of Great Britain is a history of repeated injuries and usurpations, all having in direct object the establishment of an absolute Tyranny over these States. To prove this, let Facts be submitted to a candid world.

1. He has refused his Assent to Laws, the most wholesome and necessary for the public good.

2. He has forbidden his Governors to pass Laws of immediate and pressing importance, unless suspended in their operation till his Assent should be obtained; and when so suspended, he has utterly neglected to attend to them.

3. He has refused to pass other Laws for the accommodation of large districts of people, unless those people would relinquish the right of Representation in the Legislature, a right inestimable to them and formidable to tyrants only.

4. He has called together legislative bodies at places unusual, uncomfortable, and distant from the depository of their public Records, for the sole purpose of fatiguing them into compliance with his measures.

He has dissolved Representative Houses repeatedly, for opposing with manly firmness his invasions on the rights of the people.

5. He has refused for a long time, after such dissolutions, to cause others to be elected; whereby the Legislative powers, incapable of Annihilation, have returned to the People at large for their exercise; the State remaining in the mean time exposed to all the dangers of invasion from without, and convulsions within.

6. He has endeavoured to prevent the population of these States; for that purpose obstructing the Laws for Naturalization of Foreigners; refusing to pass others to encourage their migrations hither, and raising the conditions of new Appropriations of Lands.

7. He has obstructed the Administration of Justice, by refusing his Assent to Laws for establishing Judiciary powers.

8. He has made Judges dependent on his Will alone, for the tenure of their offices, and the amount and payment of their salaries.

9. He has erected a multitude of New Offices, and sent hither swarms of Officers to harrass our people, and eat out their substance.

He has kept among us, in times of peace, Standing Armies without the Consent of our legislatures.

10. He has affected to render the Military independent of and superior to the Civil power.

11. He has combined with others to subject us to a jurisdiction foreign to our constitution, and unacknowledged by our laws; giving his Assent to their Acts of pretended Legislation:

For Quartering large bodies of armed troops among us:

For protecting them, by a mock Trial, from punishment for any Murders which they should commit on the Inhabitants of these States:

For cutting off our Trade with all parts of the world:

12. For imposing Taxes on us without our Consent:

For depriving us in many cases, of the benefits of Trial by Jury:

For transporting us beyond Seas to be tried for pretended offences

13. For abolishing the free System of English Laws in a neighbouring Province, establishing therein an Arbitrary government, and enlarging its Boundaries so as to render it at once an example and fit instrument for introducing the same absolute rule into these Colonies:

14. For taking away our Charters, abolishing our most valuable Laws, and altering fundamentally the Forms of our Governments:

For suspending our own Legislatures, and declaring themselves invested with power to legislate for us in all cases whatsoever.

15. He has abdicated Government here, by declaring us out of his Protection and waging War against us.

16. He has plundered our seas, ravaged our Coasts, burnt our towns, and destroyed the lives of our people.

He is at this time transporting large Armies of foreign Mercenaries to compleat the works of death, desolation and tyranny, already begun with circumstances of Cruelty & perfidy scarcely paralleled in the most barbarous ages, and totally unworthy the Head of a civilized nation.

He has constrained our fellow Citizens taken Captive on the high Seas to bear Arms against their Country, to become the executioners of their friends and Brethren, or to fall themselves by their Hands.

17. He has excited domestic insurrections amongst us, and has endeavoured to bring on the inhabitants of our frontiers, the merciless Indian Savages, whose known rule of warfare, is an undistinguished destruction of all ages, sexes and conditions.

18. In every stage of these Oppressions We have Petitioned for Redress in the most humble terms: Our repeated Petitions have been answered only by repeated injury. A Prince whose character is thus marked by every act which may define a Tyrant, is unfit to be the ruler of a free people.

19. Nor have We been wanting in attentions to our Brittish brethren. We have warned them from time to time of attempts by their legislature to extend an unwarrantable jurisdiction over us. We have reminded them of the circumstances of our emigration and settlement here. We have appealed to their native justice and magnanimity, and we have conjured them by the ties of our common kindred to disavow these usurpations, which, would inevitably interrupt our connections and correspondence. They too have been deaf to the voice of justice and of consanguinity. We must, therefore, acquiesce in the necessity, which denounces our Separation, and hold them, as we hold the rest of mankind, Enemies in War, in Peace Friends.

We, therefore, the Representatives of the united States of America, in General Congress, Assembled, appealing to the Supreme Judge of the world for the rectitude of our intentions, do, in the Name, and by Authority of the good People of these Colonies, solemnly publish and declare, That these United Colonies are, and of Right ought to be Free and Independent States; that they are Absolved from all Allegiance to the British Crown, and that all political connection between them and the State of Great Britain, is and ought to be totally dissolved; and that as Free and Independent States, they have full Power to levy War, conclude Peace, contract Alliances, establish Commerce, and to do all other Acts and Things which Independent States may of right do. And for the support of this Declaration, with a firm reliance on the protection of divine Providence, we mutually pledge to each other our Lives, our Fortunes and our sacred Honor.

The Declaration of Independence 2014 Grievances Lodged Against the United States Federal Government

We the people hold these truths to be self-evident, that our unalienable rights of Life, Liberty and the pursuit of happiness that we consented to our government to protect and bless, have come to destructive ends under the present tyrannical politicians. Therefore, it is the right of the people to alter the course of this government with a complete change of elected members in the House of Representatives and in the Senate that will abide by the law of the Constitution.

The recent history of our Presidents and members of Congress is a record of repeated offenses and takeovers, all having to do with making the Constitution null and void, for they desire to establish absolute tyranny over everybody in every avenue of life.

1. Our elected politicians refuse to assent to the Constitution, the Supreme Law of the land, that is most wholesome and necessary for *We the People's* good.

2. The Executive branch, under the guise of justice, has mandated the Justice Department to routinely block the states' right to govern under the authority of Amendment X of the U.S. Constitution.

3. Congress refuses to relinquish or reject harmful laws and regulations on every aspect of our society from the labor laws, ecology laws, Sustainable Development (Agenda 21) laws and regulations, energy laws and tax laws. They are relentless in all their endeavors to take away our Bill of Rights granted by our Constitution.

4. The President and the Democrat-controlled Congress used every coercive measure possible as they harangued, bribed, bartered and promised unattainable ideals while their media partners disparaged the people of our nation who were against them. By their defiant actions, they have created an unconstitutional law that forces everybody into the country's health care system through the ObamaCare law. Not only that, but they command that we all MUST have healthcare or else we shall be fined. And soon every doctor in the nation will be required to report our health records and force us to answer political and moral questions, and answers will be given to the government.

5. The President and his followers as well as Congress as a whole, will not protect us from the invasion of terrorists on our southern border while they relish every fanatical action or deadly event that they purposely use to further take away our Constitutional rights.

6. Congress refuses passage of immigration laws that will benefit all the people. The President continually obstructs the laws of states and even refuses to abide by the laws that exist.

7. Congress has been unwilling to act on their own Constitutional authority to balance the power of the executive branch which would require the president to abide by the Constitution. This lack of balance is because Congress itself refuses to abide by the Constitution. They infringe and abridge the amendments through unconstitutional legislation and tyrannically rule over the States.

8. Congress did not stop or condemn the President when he went to coerce the Supreme Court Judge to rule in favor of the President's unconstitutional healthcare bill.

9. Congress and the executive branch are daily adding new, unelected government employees giving them the authority to interpret bills passed, then create new regulations and rules based upon their whims and notions and thereby harass the citizens with swarms of officials that force us to obey or suffer monetary damage.

10. Congress has affected to render our military independent of the local militia provided in the Constitution. Meanwhile, they have created armed forces with firearms that are greatly more powerful than the firearms they allow *We the People* to own. And daily, most of our politicians at the state and federal level relentlessly attempt to take away the guns we have.

11. The Constitution only allows Congress to make the laws, yet Congress allows the decisions of judges to be the law of the land. Congress will not punish these judges by removing them from the court after such a ruling nor will they reprimand any judge that studies foreign laws in order to make a judgment in our country where they are sworn to uphold ONLY the U.S. Constitution.

12. Congress and the President have imposed a tremendously huge debt on us without our consent and then they force us to pay even higher taxes.

13. Congress, in Article I section 8 of the Constitution, has the power to make rules and regulations in only 18 areas of management; their legislative power is limited to only those areas. However, they have found ways to coerce *We the People* and the state governments into believing they must help us live and do business in every state by offering huge sums of our taxpayer money as incentive for their tyranny.

14. The cities, the states and Congress refuse to abide by our U.S. Constitution as these government entities illegally take away our right to bear arms as we travel across this great nation. Every city, every county and every state infringes on our right to carry and bear arms as each of them pass different unconstitutional laws that contradict the Constitution.

15. Congress has abdicated its authority to the Executive Branch of our government. Therefore, all elected congressional members over the decades are responsible for the deaths of our citizens at Ruby Ridge, at Waco Texas and on the border. Our Supreme law of the land, our Constitution, is not obeyed. There are no principles followed except the politician's ideologies. The unconstitutional gun laws, the unconstitutional creation of the FBI; the illegal powers given to the Executive branch and the President's Alcohol Tobacco and Firearms division are just a few examples of the government's ever-growing tentacles of tyranny.

16. Under the pretense of the rule of Constitutional law, the President and Congress deny oil and gas drilling that destroys our coastal oil-based industry. Knowingly they continue to ruin the livelihood of the people along our nation's coastline; they allow searches and seizures of our nation's businesses for no given reason; they see nothing wrong when people's lands and bank accounts are seized; they have no concern for the prosperity of our nation's farmers while they allow orders that take away their irrigation water. *We the People* are not under the rule of the Constitution, but under rule of tyrants.

17. Our President, along with a large number of his crony politicians, arouses domestic dissension among our citizens; between the rich and poor, between the conservatives and liberals, between the Republicans and Democrats, between the races, between religions and between gun owners and those people whose emotions are traumatized by gun deaths. Bent on tyranny, they use any means possible to use any traumatic event and destructive words, all with the sole purpose to cause further erosion of our freedoms and liberties.

18. Judges at the state and federal level overrule the people-approved initiatives and make rulings on matters that create new laws. The only supreme law is their decisions and with the abdication of Congress; they have tyrannical, unconstitutional power.

19. We have reminded, we have appealed, we have cried out with loud voices of reason about these offences to those we have voted in as our employees, yet they will not listen and have become tyrants over *We the People* as they abuse us with ever-increasing control over our lives.

God Created Our Founding Fathers

America Today and Tomorrow

Are you content to merely go about your normal everyday hectic life and allow our national government in Washington D. C. to control your children from birth to the grave? Are you convinced that you can do nothing to help stop those in government from your city to state and national level? Will you be able to say with conviction that you did all that you could do to save your children's and grandchildren's Constitutional freedoms?

No matter if you can answer yes or no, I encourage you to read the novel *2020 Torn Asunder* and you will see with 2020 vision what your future will be by the year 2020. No matter if you feel helpless and hopeless in the political world you must get involved in the political realm of our country and help save our liberties or you will be cast into the coming evil consequences predicted by our founders and depicted in my novel.

After your read *2020 Torn Asunder* and come to the realization that you will have a troublesome future—have no fear—this small Constitutional book will help save our Constitution if you join together in electing new people to public office. I hope the words of our Founding Fathers will convince you to get involved now, and begin to defend our remaining freedoms that will soon be gone.

Our Founding Fathers

In the beginning when God made Earth, he told man to manage the affairs of his own people, and from that day forward man dominated fellow man. There arose brutal Pharaohs, tyrant Kings, authoritarian Caesars, intolerant church Popes, evil dictators and ruthless Tribal Chiefs. Almost daily these authoritarian, intolerant, evil rulers dictated new regulations and laws upon the people who faced the punishment of prison or death if they did not obey. Debtors were condemned to prison, babies killed, women sacrificed and Christians slaughtered or fed to wild beasts. Most people owned nothing. If they had businesses or farms they only survived if they paid off the corrupt politicians. The common people did not control the food supply. They had no weapons to repel the government's armies that took their land, their houses and all the gold. The people begged, stole, perished or relied on their government's promises of help if they obeyed every law or regulation and reelect the same politicians back into office.

After thousands of years of government corruption throughout the world, God again looked down on Earth and saw that there was a grave need to save mankind from the dictates of godless rulers. In His foreknowledge he saw a country that would throw off the bonds of their intolerant ruler, but he needed a few brave men that could change the world. And so He created our Founding Fathers who in 1776 declared the United States free from the tyranny of King George III.

There never had been a limited government ruled by the people.

There never had been men, women and children free to worship God.

There never were a free people who owned land without the fear of their rulers taking it from them.

Never had mankind owned businesses free of government controls.

Never on earth did a people have the freedom to speak their opinions without the fear of punishment.

Never had a people of any country been blessed with Domestic Tranquility just knowing that their personal belongings were secure from their government's seizure. And at the time of mankind's last chance to receive his God-endowed unalienable rights to life, liberty and the pursuit of happiness, God created our Founding Fathers.

Never had a people been given the unhindered freedom to write their thoughts and opinions.

Never on the Earth had any people been free of the fear of their government that on a whim would send them to prison.

Never in the history of mankind did man freely assemble together and not worry about their government's intrusion and their sudden capture and imprisonment.

Never had the common people had the right to bear arms equal to their ruler's armies.

God knew He needed a free people to show the world how He wanted a government to operate and God created our virtuous God-fearing Founders: Thomas Jefferson, Benjamin Franklin, George Washington, Alexander Hamilton, James Madison, John and Samuel Adams, Roger Sherman, John Dickinson, George Mason, William Patterson, Benjamin Rush, and many others.

God knew that *We the People* needed bold moral men and women to fight for the cause of liberty. He needed statesmen and stateswomen to fight for a government that would provide a common defense, Domestic Tranquility and the Blessings of Liberty. Therefore, God created our Founding Fathers with wisdom; and with God's help the U.S. Constitution became the Supreme law of the Land.

God foresaw that no government had ever functioned for the people's peaceful general welfare. He also knew that if government's role was unlimited over the people it would be evil men dominating fellow man. Therefore, He ordained our Founding Fathers who created the Constitution with only 18 functions for the House of Representatives, with limited set functions for the Senate, with the President restricted to only certain powers and the judicial branch of the government with definite restrictions.

And at long last, God looked down on the planet Earth, and He was satisfied with the federal government. He, via the fearless, moral, God-fearing Founding Fathers, had created the Constitution that provided the freedom of speech, the freedom to peaceably assemble, the freedom to worship, the right to bear arms wherever they went and be secure in their person, houses, papers and effects against unreasonable searches and seizures.

Yes, God knew mankind's needs, and he duly ordained the United States government that our Founding Fathers knew could only survive if the people remained a virtuous, moral, God-fearing people. God told our Founding Fathers that an immoral people and corrupt leaders could and would destroy what they with God's help had created. **And it happened!**

In this year of 2014, God again sees that corrupt, immoral politicians have thrown aside the U.S. Constitution and they dominate fellow man.

Our Founding Fathers would turn over in their graves if they knew that the Constitution is no longer the Supreme law of the land. If they could—they would arise and fight to save our Constitution. They would turn to God and pray for guidance and ask for *We the People* to turn from our wicked ways and once again be a virtuous and moral people. But—they cannot.

Therefore, it is up to us to stand in the gap created by the centuries of time. It is up to *We the People* to return to God's plan that calls for all people to live a virtuous, moral life.

One more time God looks down on Earth and He sees everyone in the world under the control of tyrants. Once again, in the United States of America, men and women dominate fellow humanity with hundreds of thousands of rules starting at the local level up to what is supposed to be a federal government. And as in 1776, God needs men and women who will do as our Founding Fathers did—stand up and demand that we be governed by the Constitution, the Supreme rule of the land. *We the People* need present day Founding Fathers and Mothers. We must vote into office at every level of government only statesmen and stateswomen that vow to abide by the Constitution and then do it!

John Adams told us; *"Be not intimidated... nor suffer yourselves to be wheedled out of your liberties by any pretense of politeness, delicacy, or decency. These, as they are often used, are but three different names for hypocrisy, chicanery and cowardice"*

I Ask a Few Simple Questions

Is it possible for God to create people who can be as our Founding Fathers? Are you prepared to stand up and with fearlessness, speak the truth? Will you tell the nation that if they do not return to God and vote out the corrupt politicians, that they will be doomed to poverty and oppression?

Thomas Jefferson warned us: *"All tyranny needs to gain a foothold is for people of good conscience to remain silent."*

It may be too late, for our politicians at every level have already TORN ASUNDER the Constitution. But—I pray for thirty-to-fifty thousand men or women who will take a stand as our Founding Fathers did and dare to fight for liberty as we boldly attempt to save our Constitution even as hateful, corrupt, tyrannical people try to destroy us with lies, deceit, derision and disparagement. Let us rally together*! 'Let's Save Our Constitution!'* We need to stir up those who are silent!

I use Frederick Douglass's words that amply apply to our country today. *"It is not light that is needed, but fire; it is not the gentle shower, but thunder. We need the storm, the whirlwind and the earthquake. The feeling of the nation must be quickened; the conscience of the nation must be roused; the propriety of the nation must be startled; the hypocrisy of the nation must be exposed; its crimes against God and man must be proclaimed and denounced."*

We must inform the ignorant! We must teach the Constitution to the uninformed! I plead for you to join the battle to save our country from injustice! Let's Save Our Constitution from the Tyrants that have already torn it asunder!

I ask one last question:

Does God Still Create Brave Men and Women?

'Let's Save Our Constitution!'
Let Freedom Ring!